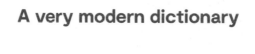

A very modern dictionary

A very modern dictionary

Tobias Anthony

Introduction

Welcome, friends, to *A Very Modern Dictionary*. This handy guidebook will help you to navigate the confusing and bewildering beast that is the ever-changing English language. Any dictionary is charged with the task of conveying and accurately representing language in its various stages of evolution – for language is in a constant state of flux, always moving and shifting and blending. The transformation of language can often defy logic. Contemporary usage of 'literally' is a perfect case study: the word has now come to replace the word 'figuratively', despite its original meaning being the polar opposite. It's small joys, such as this, which make studying linguistics and etymology (the origin of words) endlessly enjoyable. They can also render the English language a complete nightmare if you stop paying attention, even for just a second.

This dictionary ventures through the deepest and dankest corners of the internet to bring you an accurate sense of how language is used online. Sure, it's a shitshow of hyperbole and neologism that would make Shakespeare hang his head in shame. But that's the world in which we communicate, so we best keep up, right?

In these pages you'll find everything from shrewd portmanteaus and onomatopoeia to initialisms and acronyms, nouns and verbs, and, of course, some utterly nonsensical slang popularised by social media and reality television. Here, it's crucial to note that many of the most beloved phrases in this book originate from communities that are predominately people of colour and/or queer people of colour. The adjectival use of the word 'lit' comes to mind, as does the shrieking battle cry of 'yass queen' – both staples of the contemporary white teenager's lexicon. We seek not to contribute to this cultural misappropriation, but rather to celebrate modern language in all its messy glory. We hope you'll enjoy this celebration, too.

As you flick through over 600 entries in this book, one crucial fact will become clear: context is everything. User discretion is vital in making many of these words and phrases shine. To any parents reading this book, maybe you'll tap into some 'woke' lingo that you can use front of your kid's friends, as a fun surprise! And, for any teenagers reading, you might gift this book to your parents and highlight certain phrases you'd rather they refrain from using in the company of your friends. Either way, turn the page and come on in! Let us shine an iPhone light on the many modern words and phrases that will help you speak and type in the language of our time.

A

4chan
noun
A website where users can post images anonymously. It has gained notoriety for its involvement with several internet pranks, memes, as well as for its connection to subcultures, online activist groups, and alt-right sympathisers.

420
phrase
Unsubtle code for the consumption of cannabis. On social and dating apps, the phrase '420 friendly' means you're a pot smoker, or at least open to it. It suggests that 4:20pm is the most socially acceptable time to spark a joint.

AAMOF
initialism
As a matter of fact.

-ability
suffix
Indicates the degree to which something is suitable or capable. Is tacked on to just about any old word in a manner of reckless neology. (See also: **marketability**, **viewability**, and **relatability**.)

ad blocker
noun
Software designed to prevent advertisements from appearing on a website. Ad blockers are a welcome resource to help fend off the reality that, through targeted advertising, Google can see deep into your personal data, maybe even your soul... But hey, ignorance is bliss.

ADIH
initialism
Another day in hell.

ADN
initialism
Any day now.

adorkable
adjective
Portmanteau of *adorable* and *dork*. Someone socially inept, clumsy, and/or with commonly perceived 'geeky' interests, like video games or comic books, but who is also aesthetically adorable (at least, in the eye of the beholder).

adulting
verb
To perform tasks commonly associated with the responsibilities or duties expected of an adult. If your weekend plans include home repairs, filing your taxes, and/or other essential life admin, then you've got some serious *adulting* to do.

AEAP
initialism
As early as possible.

AF
initialism
Initialism of *as fuck*; meaning 'intensely so': *Damn, that exam was hard AF.*

AFAIK
acronym / initialism
As far as I know.

AFAIR
acronym / initialism
As far as I remember or as far as I recall.

AKA
initialism
Also known as. Necessary for wrestling, or any other profession in which stage names are a necessity: Dwayne Johnson, AKA The Rock.

ALAP
acronym / initialism
As late as possible. This is *ASAP*'s lazier, acronymic cousin. It's employed when you're a slow-moving sloth or just really, really disinterested in... *everything*.

AMA
initialism
Ask me anything. Now here's an initialism with the propensity to backfire...

amirite?
phrase
Contraction of *am I right?* Usually affirmatory, and essentially asking, 'Agreed?'. Sometimes deployed rhetorically to confirm the speaker's own opinion: *Bey's new track is straight-up fire, amirite?* Meaning: 'Beyoncé Knowles-Carter has the best new musical release, and I'm right to say so, because it is true.'

ancient grains
noun
A variety of food sources including quinoa, chia, amaranth, millet, and wild rice, as well as some forms of wheat including spelt and farro. Essentially a marketing term used to imbue these grains and pseudo-cereals with an air of romanticism and mysticism to make them appear more nutritious and bougie.

and scene
phrase
A reference to a statement a dramatic actor might say at the conclusion of a performance, typically at the end of a monologue. In day-to-day usage, it's a sign-off indicating the momentous nature (ironically or otherwise) of what you've said or done: *Aaaand scene...*

A

apology tour
noun
The apologies made (most typically) by celebrities on various social media and news media platforms following public outcry over a controversial comment or action. Necessitated by the rights of every social media user to express their extreme and impassioned outrage, and their subsequent need for immediate placation.

as
adverb
Emphasising the degree to which something *is*, this adverb is common to Australia and New Zealand. When applied to the end of an adjective, it heightens the preceding word: *easy as*, meaning 'very easy'; *hard as*, meaning 'very hard'; or *busy as*, meaning 'the location was really fucking crowded'.

ASAP
acronym / initialism
As soon as possible. A classic! The choice is yours: say the letters individually, or pronounce as one singular word.

ASL
initialism
Age, sex, location? The OG internet pickup line. Don't you remember using this one in your first chatroom?

ASMR
initialism
Standing for 'autonomous sensory meridian response', it is most common today to hear ASMR referred to in context with ASMR videos, which are a popular category of YouTube. ASMR videos are designed to help viewers relax, and include soft and constant noises, such as the sound of people eating or gently whispering.

ATM
initialism
At the moment. Common in all digital communication. No, Grandpa, it has nothing to do with an automated teller machine. Who even uses cash anymore?

at the end of the day
phrase
The true point of contention or the point being made. Employed when highlighting your meaning in a conversation, usually when concluding a subject: *We could sit around and talk politics for hours, but, at the end of the day, I'll never regret voting for Bernie.*

attention whore
noun
Someone who will do anything for attention, or any person, regardless of gender, who seeks out attention – both good and bad – willingly.

awkies
adjective
This is an abbreviation of the word 'awkward' only a thousand times cuter. This is awks' adorable cousin. (See 'awks', below.)

awks
abbreviation / adjective
This is an abbreviation of the word 'awkward', and therefore carries its same meaning. Generally, however, this term suggests a feeling of uneasy embarrassment (as opposed to hard or difficult): *Seeing my accountant is going to be a little awks after we matched on Tinder...*

AYSOS
acronym / initialism
Are you stupid or something? A valid question: *So, you bought this book... AYSOS?*

B3
initialism
Blah, blah, blah. That's right, three times the blah! *She was telling me all kinds of things about her vacation and B3...*

B4
initialism
Before. No, not after. Before.

B4YKI
initialism
Before you know it: *She was chatting about her vacation and B4YKI, Jenny's telling me she's getting divorced!* (See, you have to pay attention to these kinds of conversations, you can't just tune out and *B3* and miss all the *tea.*)

bae
acronym / noun
Acronym for *before anyone else*, and a
shortened term for babe or baby; usually
used to describe a significant other or a
best friend: *Props to bae for whipping up
a bomb chicken and veggie keto soup.*

bafflegab
noun
Portmanteau of *baffling* and *gab*; any
incomprehensible or pretentious verbiage,
but most especially bureaucratic speech.

baller
adjective / noun
A rockstar, someone with confidence and swag.
Originating from sports terms like footballer or
basketballer, words associated with icons who
exude coolness. Also describes something
impressive: *You bought three dozen tequila shots?
Damn. That's baller.*

Bank of Mom and Dad
noun
Describes a grown-up who remains financially supported by their parents: *Taking a loan from the Bank of Mum and Dad*. Generally used as a derisive statement aimed at millennials supported in their early adult years by their Generation X parents. Unsurprisingly, it is the same Gen Xers who are attributed with coining the phrase.

basic
adjective
Devoid of any characteristics that make a person in any way interesting; specifically pertaining to tastes and interests deemed beige, bland, and boring: *Eugh, all they ever talk about is scented candles and getting Aperol Spritzes after work. Sooooo basic, amirite?*

bb
abbreviation
Short for 'baby'.

BBL
initialism
Be back later.

BD
initialism
Big deal. Is there a better way to sound bitchy on the internet than by dropping a BD? Nope.

BDE
initialism
Shorthand for 'big dick energy', BDE refers to a certain cocksure attitude: in other words, confidence without arrogance. The kind of vibe (or energy) a person is likely to give off when they know they've got the full package: *John Hamm reeks of BDE*.

B(ad)DE
initialism
Short for 'bad dick energy', B(ad)DE can also be used to refer to someone riddled with insecurities. When you're getting that kind of B(ad)DE from your Tinder date, then it's time to orchestrate a 'family emergency' phone call.

beat face
noun
When someone has a 'beat face', it doesn't mean any awful thing you might suspect. In fact, it means someone has a face full of makeup. And not just any kind of makeup either, a *flawless* look. The kind that turns anyone into a goddamn diva.

Becky with the good hair
phrase
A lyric taken from Beyoncé's track 'Sorry', from the iconic album *Lemonade*, which has come to mean 'the other woman'.

bee-tee-dubs
phrase
The latest way to stylise *BTW*, an initialism of *by the way*. Not only is it longer to type, it's also completely idiotic, which is why everyone in the group chat is doing it: *Bee-tee-dubs you guys, I'm kinda feeling like hitting happy hour tonight?!?*

believe that
phrase
Meaning 'it's true', only with one hundred times the *chutzpah*. Employed at the end of a statement to let people know that there is no denying what you've just said: *If King Kong were around today, I'm sure I could kick his ass. Believe that.*

BF
initialism / noun
Short for 'boyfriend': *Me and the BF are totes excited to come see you after our CrossFit sesh tomorrow!* (See also: **GF**.)

BFF
initialism / noun
Inititialism of *best friend forever*; that special someone in your life who you would do almost anything for. While your BFF can also be your BF or GF, this is rarely the context in which this is employed, as it generally only refers to non-romantic relationships.

bieee
exclamation
An alternative spelling for 'goodbye' or 'bye'. It remains a farewell, but all those extra, high-pitched e's just make it much happier and fun. Think about it, how would you rather have someone say 'goodbye' to you? (See also. hieee.)

bi-line
noun
The degree to which someone is bisexual. A metaphorical line where your sexuality starts to be less clearly defined. Everyone has a bi-line, but not everybody has crossed it. Discovering your bi-line can be greatly assisted by the consumption of tequila.

bingeable
adjective
Something that can be *binged* (see below), especially relating to television: *Did you catch the season on Netflix? So bingeable!*

binged
verb
The act of consuming large amounts of audiovisual content in a single period of time: *I binged the new season of* Stranger Things *in one night. Whoops.*

bleeding edge
noun
The leading edge of the leading edge. Something so devastatingly new and advanced that saying 'cutting edge' just won't suffice.

body positivity / bodypos
phrase / noun
A progressive movement encouraging acceptance of body types that sit outside the narrow parameters of those promoted in mainstream culture. Being body positive is another way of saying we don't all look like models or celebrities, and that's okay!

boho
adjective / noun
Shorthand for 'Bohemian', boho can be a person or aesthetic that is socially unconventional.

boo
noun
Not what you yell when jumping out from behind a door, now a pet name for your significant other. Your boo is your lover and BFF all in one. A little like bae, only not. It's *boo*.

bop
abbreviation / noun
Used in reference to pop songs, 'bop' is short for 'bopper', meaning a song that is really good: *Billie Eilish's new track is a bop*.

booch
abbreviation / noun
The far cooler way of saying kombucha, the coolest drink of all.

boomer
abbreviation / adjective / noun
Short for 'Baby Boomer', boomer has become a derogatory term referencing certain unpopular traits associated with that generation, such as an indifference to the inevitable demise of the planet caused by the environmental havoc wreaked by humankind.

bougie
adjective
Derived from the word 'bourgeois', which refers to people who are upper-class and representative of certain values – materialistic and conservative, generally speaking. In slang today, *however, 'bougie' is another word for 'fancy': Let's go out for a bougie brunch, or, OMFG all I want is a bougie juice to cure this hangover.*

bounce
verb
To 'bounce' means to leave suddenly and deliberately: *This party blows. Let's bounce.*

boyfriends of Instagram
noun
The men behind the camera! For every great shot of an adorable human on Instagram there is a man being forced into a compromised position to manufacture that Insta-worthy moment. A better noun might be 'human selfie-stick'.

BRB
initialism / phrase
Initialism of *be right back*, commonly employed in digital conversations when one person needs to be away from their screen or mobile device for a moment and wants to convey their intention to return: *Need to use the bathroom... brb.*

bread
noun
Cash money; income: *Let's get this morning, fam. Gonna see some bread today!* (See also: **paper**.)

bro code
noun
The understanding between bros regarding agreed upon actions and reactions to a variety of subjects and situations. For instance, the bro code stipulates that should a bro meet a particularly attractive companion at a party, you leave him alone regardless of the situation. If this bro drove you to the party and you need to leave, then you need to find your own way home without him.

broga
noun
Yoga for bros!

bromance
noun / portmanteau
Portmanteau of *bro* and *romance*. A deep, platonic, non-sexual relationship between two men.

BRT
initialism
Be right there.

bruh?
exclamation
An exclamation of sorts, 'bruh?' is shorthand for 'seriously?' It's what you say when something is dumb or ridiculous and worthy of derision.
Ted: *I know it's 2020, but I still can't stop listening to Coldplay.*
Nelly: *Bruh?*

BTAIM
initialism
Be that as it may.

BTW
initialism / phrase
By the way. About as commonly used now as 'FYI' (for your information).

burn
noun / verb
An accurate and/or witty criticism
deemed so incisive that it leaves you
with no ability to reply. Sometimes, for
added emphasis, referred to as an *ice
burn*, to indicate the cold-heartedness
of the insult.

Bye, Felicia.
phrase
Used to express total disinterest at the
departure of someone detestable and/or
insignificant, originating from the 1995 Ice
Cube movie *Friday*: *Sho completely blanked
me when I tried to neg her, so I was all like,
'bye, Felicia'*. (See also: **Damn, Gina**.)

cancel
verb
To reject something. You can cancel a person, place, or thing: *You don't like Jenny because she's annoying? Just go ahead and cancel that girl from your life.* You don't feel like doing your homework? *Don't worry, your homework is cancelled, forget it.* (See also: **deplatform**.)

can't even...
phrase
Signifies incomprehension or being indisposed, or a combination thereof. Meaning that you either cannot wrap your mind around something because it is too stupid or too cute, or that you cannot deal with something, either because it would pain you to or because you're not in the right frame of mind: *I'm laughing so hard, I literally can't even*, or, *WTF was that all about? I can't even...*

catfish
noun / verb
A person who pretends to be somebody else online,
either by hacking into someone's social media accounts
or by creating false accounts under a fake identity. The
term was coined in Henry Joost and Ariel Schulman's
2010 documentary *Catfish*.

#checkyourprivilege
hashtag
An attachment to a social media post intended
to draw attention to the privileges of people
from Western capitalist societies, most especially
those who make up the middle-class majority.
Unfortunately, now commonly misappropriated by
that same group and used as a way to defuse what
is clearly an insufferable humblebrag: *Embracing
that #boholife for the rest of the holidays with
my #messyhair and #lazymornings. Whatever
you do, do it with your whole #spirit. #wanderlust
#checkyourprivilege.* (See also: **humble brag**.)

chopped and screwed
phrase
To change drastically. Originally used to refer to
the remixing of hip-hop music: *That fire track got
chopped and screwed*. Now commonly used in a
broader context with regard to inebriation: *I went
out on the weekend and got completely chopped
and screwed*.

#chosen
hashtag
A social media hashtag commonly used to describe a state of smug enlightenment and a sense of feeling hand-picked by a deity for a specified task, or being selected by fate to experience good fortune: *Just got the last keto bar at my fav brunch spot! #chosen.*

chronotype
noun
Behavioural classification based on underlying circadian rhythms. A person's propensity to sleep at a particular time during a twenty-four-hour period. In other words, a fancy, sciency way of saying whether or not you are a morning person.

cis / cisgender
adjective
Those who identify as the gender they were assigned at birth. *Cis* is Latin for 'on this side of'.

clapback
noun
A clapback is a comeback. Not of the artistic- or athletic-career kind, but the verbal kind of comeback. A retort that's filled with attitude – it's one that is sassy, one that throws shade: *Vince called Michaela an idiot in class today. You should've heard her clapback. Damn!*

C

clickbait

noun

A sensational online headline (or combination of headline and image) that is very carefully constructed to rouse your curiosity and manipulate you into clicking on a link. Specifically deployed to increase page views and hence generate online-advertising revenue.

clusterfuck

noun

An event of a disastrous nature, something that was extremely difficult or went badly: *Yesterday, absolutely everything that could go wrong, did go wrong; it was an utter clusterfuck.*

clutch

adjective / noun

The ability to perform under pressure – in 'the clutch'. *Clutch* can be used more broadly to describe any fortuitous moment, however: *You're walking down the street bummed out because you've just paid your rent and your ass is broke. A fifty-dollar bill drifts past on the sidewalk. You pick it up... clutch.*

clutching pearls
phrase / verb
A moment of shock or surprise so strong that the person brings their hand to their chest as if grabbing for a pearl necklace that isn't there: *When you go see Jordan Peele's new movie, y'all be clutching pearls.*

Columbusing
verb
When white people claim to have 'discovered' something that has been long known by non-white people. Originating from *College Humor*, it refers to explorer Christopher Columbus's 'discovery' of the Americas, despite the fact that the significant native populations were already quite aware of their own existence.

conscious uncoupling
phrase
What you call a breakup when you don't want to call a breakup a breakup... *We didn't break up. It was a conscious uncoupling.* The origins of this phrase hark back to a simpler time, when Coldplay's Chris Martin and actor Gwyneth Paltrow announced their amicable split.

content
noun
Creative material, such as writing, photography, animation, or video, required to feed the insatiable appetites of internet users (AKA *everybody*). Those who produce this online content even call themselves *content creators*, as opposed to writers, photographers, animators, filmmakers, etc.

cooked
adjective
Much like the word 'baked', which means 'stoned', cooked has come to mean being high, though usually as the result of taking amphetamines. It can also be used to describe *clusterfuck*-like situations.

correct
adjective / phrase
Right beyond a shadow of a doubt; perfect. Commonly employed with regard to how you present yourself and how you look. If you *come correct*, then you are looking sharp or on point. (See also: **on point**.)

covfefe
???
'Despite the constant negative press *covfefe*.'

co-working space
noun
Space in which individuals or groups of people from various companies work together in an office-like environment. Most commonly found in converted warehouse spaces with interior design features such as exposed brick walls, ping pong table, craft beer fridge, and inspiring mural by a local street artist.

crine
abbreviation / verb
An alternative spelling for 'crying' and its abbreviation 'cryin'': *For crine out loud!*

CSL
initialism
Can't stop laughing.

CTN
initialism
Can't talk now.

cuffing season
noun
In the coldest months of the year, people have a tendency to get a little lonely. For singles, this is the season to get 'cuffed', which is another way of saying 'tied down' by or 'bound' to someone else. With that extra time spent indoors, this is the time of year to start a relationship...

Cumberbitches
noun
Fans of British actor and thespian Benedict Cumberbatch.

cut to
noun / phrase
Taken from film language, to 'cut to' anything means a jump in time. When telling a story, for instance: *Remember Jill, from high school? I ran into her on the street, like, three weeks ago. Cut to: us getting engaged in Maui.*

CW
initialism / noun
An initialism for 'content warning', this is to flag that something contains certain materials, especially those of an explicit nature, that might offend some viewers, readers, or listeners, depending on the context. (See also: **trigger warning** and **UV**.)

CWOT
initialism
Complete waste of time.

cyberbullying
verb
To harass, hurt, and/or offend someone online, generally via social media platforms. Usually refers to the harassment of children and teenagers, but adults can be cyberbullied, too, we just don't like to call it that because we like to pretend that adults are more sophisticated than children. (See also: **troll**)

CYT
initialism
See you tomorrow.

dabbing / the dab
noun / verb
Dabbing or 'the dab' is a kind of dance move or gesture popularised in meme culture. The action involves dropping one's head into the crook of one's elbow while holding that arm (the right) at an upwardly slanted angle, while the other arm (the left) is raised out in the same direction at a parallel to the other. It almost looks like the person has begun sneezing while attempting a Nazi salute, but... well...

dad
noun
We all know what a dad is: one's father. But the word can be coopted for general usage, carrying with it the very best connotations of fatherhood. A 'dad', in this new context, is a role model, someone reliable, someone to be admired: *Jerry's a good guy. He's a real dad.*

dad bod
noun
A complimentary description used by those attracted to a man's body that is mostly lacking in muscle definition and may rock a little bit of a paunch: *John looks so great since he stopped going to the gym. He's got a total dad bod now.*

DAE
initialism
Does anyone know?

dafuq
abbreviation / phrase
Abbreviation of *what the fuck?*; mostly the result of internet memes, where the original phrase has been shortened, joined, and spelled uniquely: *'You're a wizard, Harry...' 'Dafuq?'*

Damn, Gina.
phrase
Acknowledgement and/or approval of somebody doing or saying something impressive that you like: *'Did you see Callum get up and twerk onstage??' 'Damn, Gina!'*

dank
adjective
Of high quality, especially in reference to cannabis, memes, and fried food: *Kind sir, I would like to know from whence I might procure that dank herb?*

dank memes
noun
Memes that are dank! Dank memes are generally those in which the comedic element has been overdone, to the extent where they are excessively ironic and/or nonsensical.

dark web
noun
Part of the internet that is accessible only by way of special software that allows users to remain both anonymous and untraceable. You've probably heard of the dark web in some spy thriller, but it's very much a real thing.

dead
adjective
1. When a celebrity is 'burnt' or 'slain' by another celebrity (via a tweet or a social media attack), that celebrity dies socially and is *dead*; 2. When someone makes you laugh so hard it practically kills you, you might want to stop their joking around by saying *OMG, I'm dead!*; 3. When a trend or cultural zeitgeist is officially 'over', it is pronounced *dead*.

deadass
adverb
Rather than say 'dead serious', try saying deadass instead. This new term can be a replacement of 'for real': *I'm deadass getting this deep-fried cheeseburger, aiiight?*

defs
abbreviation
Shorthand for 'definitely': *'Are you going to check out the new Tina Fey movie?' 'Defs.'*

deplatform
verb
In the world of social media, to be deplatformed is to be, in some way, dethroned. It means one can be taken off any digital or media platform used to deliver messages to their audience. For example, someone being abusive on Twitter might be deplatformed, meaning that their access to that service will be denied. (See also: **cancel**.)

derp
noun / phrase
Used to highlight someone's mistake, whether an action or, more commonly, an idiotic statement: *'Global warming ain't real. I mean, yeah, sure, it's hotter this time of year than ever before, but it sure ain't real.' 'Derp.'*

DGA
initialism
Don't go anywhere.

DGAF
acronym / initialism
Don't give a fuck. It might look like DGA, but the F is crucial here. Don't get these two confused.

digital detox
noun
A period of time spent away from all electronic screens. Necessary from time to time in the digital world!

DIKU
initialism
Don't I know you? One can only wonder where you've gotten to online when you find yourself typing these letters...

dime
noun
A very attractive person.

DKDC
initialism
Don't know, don't care...

DL
initialism
Initialism of *down low*; something that needs to be kept quiet and/or secret: *I hear Rebecca is pregnant, but you gotta keep that on the DL.* (See also: **low key**.)

DM
initialism
Direct message. *Give me a follow, so I can DM you.* (See also: **slide into your DMs.**)

DNC
initialism
Does not compute.

DOC
initialism
Drug of choice.

doe
adverb
Though. We're not sure how this works, it just does. It's just another thing that exists today, so make your peace and move on. Examples: We are providing no examples. This makes no sense. Don't use this word.

doggo
noun
Why simply say 'dog', when you could say 'doggo'? By no stretch of the imagination is this the cutest and most fun way to refer to your canine compadre.

doing the most
phrase
A way to describe someone who goes above and beyond, in a situation requiring very little effort. Often deployed in frustration that an overachiever is making the collective look bad, or when someone's flirt game is completely shameless. (See also: **extra**.)

done
adjective
To have reached your limit with any activity or thing. *Eugh, that's it, I'm done!* Usually this term is delivered as a means of expressing exasperation, frustration, and/or exhaustion.

dope
adjective
Extremely cool and relevant. Ironically, however, the word itself is beginning to lose a bit of its dopeness... It might soon be time to drop this one, so use it while you still can!

douche / douchebag
noun
Obnoxious idiot; could be a colleague you can't stand or that person who won't stop trolling you online.

D

dox / doxxed
verb
When someone's personal information is intentionally leaked online, they have been 'doxxed'. This has dangerous, potentially life-threatening implications, and is definitely not a cute prank. (See also: **troll**.)

Dr Google
noun
Using the internet (Google, specifically) to self-diagnose health issues. Generally considered an extremely bad idea: *'I'm pretty sure I have septicemia. I heard that elbow pain is a symptom of septicemia...' 'Really? Did Dr Google tell you that?'*

drag
verb
To rake someone over the coals; to put someone on blast: *Someone cuts in front of you in a line, you need to drag that mother to the ground.* (See also: **on blast**.)

drank
adjective
The effect following the consumption of a cough syrup containing codeine and promethazine. A state not unlike being drunk, and highly sought after by some.

dreams
interjection
An affirmative statement, expressing approval and delight, similar to 'good idea' or 'good call': *'I'm thinking I might try the cheesecake.' 'Dreams, man. Dreams.'*

drop a pin
verb
A method of sharing your location digitally. So long as you have a smartphone, simply open Google Maps and, you got it, *drop a pin!*

DQMOT
initialism
Don't quote me on this.

DTF
initialism
When you're feeling that yearning, deep in your soul, a real hankering for veggies and spices and for a nutritious, chickpea-based meal. That's when you know you're 'Down to Felafel'. Text your closest friend, if you'd like to munch falafel with some company: *Long time, no kebab! You DTF??*

duckface
noun
A face made by pushing the lips forward into a pout in order to accentuate their size, often utilised by teenage girls in selfies, and now used ironically by many selfie enthusiasts.

dudevorce
noun
The split between bros when the bromance is over. (See also: **bromance**.)

dumpster fire
noun
A disaster, something bad that nobody wants to have to deal with: *Did you see Jasper's open mic the other night? Total dumpster fire.* (See also: **garbage fire**.)

dumpster hot
adjective
A person who projects a look of simultaneous trashiness and hotness, wherein their hotness is almost amplified by their trashiness. Think, the new 'crust punk chic'.

e-cig
noun
Electronic cigarette for inhaling vaporised flavoured liquid. Usually containing a combination of nicotine, flavouring, and other chemicals, e-cigs are thought to be less harmful than traditional cigarettes and have been used by people as a step towards quitting smoking altogether. (See also: **vaping** and **juul**.)

EGOT
acronym
Emmy, Grammy, Oscar, Tony! Audrey Hepburn: Emmy, Grammy, Oscar, Tony! Whoopi Goldberg: Emmy, Grammy, Oscar, Tony! John Legend: Emmy, Grammy, Oscar, Tony! Mel Brooks, you guessed it: EGOT!

ELI5
initialism
Explain like I'm five.

emoji
noun
A pictorial alphabet used in electronic communication (mostly text messages) to express an object, idea, or emotion. There are more than one thousand different emojis, but the two most commonly used are the smiley face (☺) and the sad face (☹). The eggplant emoji might just come in third...

emoticon
noun / portmanteau
Portmanteau of *emotion* and *icon*; pictorial representations of faces using combinations of letters, numbers, and punctuation marks, which have become staples in digital conversations. The most common are those easiest to make using parentheses and semicolons or colons, including happy :), sad :(, and winking ;).

EOD
initialism
End of discussion. Or, in the professional and corporate spheres, End of day: *Daniel, I need that spreadsheet by EOD, and that's the EOD.*

EOM
initialism
End of message.

ETA
initialism
You're likely familiar with these letters meaning 'estimated time of arrival', which they do. Sometimes. But another meaning online is 'edited to add'. This is often used by bloggers when adding something to one of their posts.

extra
adjective / noun
Someone who (or something which) is trying far too hard: *Did you see Becky's new Kanye tattoo? Shit's fucking extra.* (See also: **doing the most.**)

F2F
initialism
Face to face.

face time
noun
Non-digital human interaction; face-to-face, real-world, and real-time interactions between people that are not experienced through a digital screen. So, no, a FaceTime call is not considered face time.

FACK
abbreviation
It might look like a curse word, but it isn't. FACK, in fact, stands for 'full acknowledgement'.

facts

exclamation

'Facts' is an exclamation of agreement, an affirmation. If you're in staunch support of a statement or sentiment uttered, then you may reply *Facts!*
Eloise: *This party is amazing!*
Jenny: *Facts, my dude!*

fake news

noun

You know, like, news that is fake. Or, another way of putting it: news, facts, or statistics that contravene your own opinion, ideology, agenda. Possibly the buzziest term of the decade, with only one idiotic man to blame.

fail

noun

Failure, screw-up, metaphorical car crash, disaster; generally employed in a jovial manner:
38 of the funniest fails by people who are literally the worst.

false equivalent
noun
An inaccurate analogy employed by a user in order to equate one thing with another despite these two ideas being far removed.

fam
abbreviation
Short for *family*, but generally used when addressing or referring to someone, or a group, who is not biologically related. This person is, or these people are, your found family: *What up, fam? Where my margarita at?*

fanboy / fangirl
noun
Someone who is passionate about an aspect of nerd and/or geek culture. A male who regularly attends *Star Wars* conventions would be considered a *Star Wars* fanboy.

fat-shaming
verb
The act of humiliating or criticising a person about their weight, and often falsely justified as a way to motivate people to be thinner: *Hey, bro, I wasn't fat-shaming, I was just trying to help that person get off the couch and lose those extra pounds.*

favourite / favouriting

noun / verb

When a person adds an image, song, video, or other piece of media to their list of 'favourites' online, this is the act of favouriting: *I love that picture of your cat. I'm adding it to my favourites!*

FC

initialism

Fingers crossed.

feels

noun

A feeling of extreme emotion. This is a catchall word for the emotionally inarticulate: i.e. people who use the internet way too much: *I just watched the first ten minutes of* Up. *So many feels.*

fetch

adjective

Cool. Originating from the 2004 comedy film *Mean Girls*, this term was used by the character Gretchen Wieners, who was really trying to make the word a *thing*. Despite mean girl Regina George claiming that *fetch* was never going to happen, for the ironically inclined, this term has kind of taken off in recent years.

finna

abbreviation

This word translates to 'going to' or 'will' (as in, expressing the future tense or intentions). 'Finna' is an abbreviation of 'fixing to': *I'm finna get lit tonight. I'm finna go buy a meatball sub. I'm finna gonna open up about my feelings as I trust you as a confidante.*

finesse

verb

To skillfully manipulate a person or situation, whether it be to smooth over a disagreement, or to talk someone out of their belongings: *We'd only been back at my place for five minutes before I'd finessed him out of his clothes.*

finna

abbreviation

This word translates to 'going to' or 'will' (as in, expressing the future tense or intentions). 'Finna' is an abbreviation of 'fixing to': *I'm finna get lit tonight. I'm finna go buy a meatball sub. I'm finna gonna open up about my feelings as I trust you as a confidante.*

finsta
noun / portmanteau
Combining the words 'fake' and 'Instagram',
a finsta is a person's alternative Instagram
account. A finsta is used by young
Instagrammers to avoid the prying (well,
judgemental) eyes of their parents and
extended family.

fire
adjective
The bleeding edge of cool. Fire seems
to have come to replace 'dope' in this
context: *This song is fire!* It can also work
as an alternative to the word 'lit', when lit
is being used in place of cool or dope.

First World problems
noun
Minor problems experienced by people who enjoy
the social and economic privileges of the First World;
may include issues such as being indecisive about
which restaurant to patronise, becoming irritated
about the speed of an internet service, or becoming
stressed that you don't have enough leave to cover
your six-week European vacation.

fitspo
abbreviation / portmanteau
A combination of the words 'fit' and 'inspiration'
to create 'fitspiration', 'fistpo' is then the abbreviated
form of that new word. Fitspo is an umbrella term
for images of fit and active people that claim to
inspire a healthier lifestyle.

FKA
initialism
Formerly known as: *Dwayne
Johnson, FKA The Rock*.

flavourgasm
noun / portmanteau
Portmanteau of *flavour* and *orgasm*; the
extreme delight experienced by eating food
or being introduced to a particularly good-
tasting beverage.

flex
verb
An alternative word for the act of
'showing off'. To flex isn't just about
contracting your muscles, it's to brag,
to display your 'goods', whatever they
might be. (See also: **weird flex**.)

flossing / the floss
noun / verb
Flossing or 'the floss' is a specific kind of dance in which a person repeatedly swings their arms with clenched fists in front of their body and behind, back and forth, and creates the effect of making the dancer appear to be flossing their body with a giant, imaginary piece of dental floss.

FML
abbreviation / initialism
Fuck my life... *I'm only up to the letter F?? FML.*

FOAF
initialism
Friend of a friend.

FOMO
acronym / noun
Acronym of *fear of missing out*: *I can't believe I'm not at that iPhone launch... my FOMO is peaking right now.*

footprint
noun
The outcome or cost of your existence produced via your accumulated use of resources and creation of waste. Predominantly used in regard to carbon emissions – your *carbon footprint*.

for real
phrase
An exclamation, affirmation, and/or question expressing validity or disbelief. Use is dependent on context, but the possibilities seem endless. Can be shortened to FR, so be aware: *You got 76 likes on that photo of you eating a hard-boiled egg? Are you for real?*

for the gram
phrase
To do something 'for the gram' means to engage in an activity for the sole purpose of taking pictures, which you then upload to your Instagram. Ordering a $33 kale salad, so that you can show off your healthy lifestyle online, is just one example of 'doing it for the gram'.

freegan
noun / portmanteau
Portmanteau of *free* and *vegan*; a person who eats only free, discarded food, typically from the refuse of shops or restaurants, purportedly for ecological and/or ethical reasons that has nothing to do with them just being cheapskates.

freemium
adjective / portmanteau
A pricing strategy whereby a product or service is provided for free, but money is charged for additional features. A hybrid of *free* and *premium*, usually relating to digital applications such as software and games for mobile devices.

friend zone
noun
A relationship status between two friends whereby one party is sexually and/or romantically attracted to the other, but this feeling is not reciprocated. This experience is referred to as being put in the *friend zone*.

FTW
initialism
For the win.

fuckboi
noun
Any guy who leads people into believing he's more into them than he really is, only with the sole purpose of getting them into bed. A complete and total asshat.

Fun Police
noun
Party pooper; someone who just spoils the fun: *Who died and made him the Fun Police? I was just trying to get lit, and he came up and started preaching about liver cirrhosis.*

fungry
adjective / portmanteau
Portmanteau of *fucking* and *hungry*; to be beyond mere hunger; essentially the equivalent of saying, 'I'm so hungry I could eat a horse', only much ruder and snappier.

furry
noun
A participant in the subculture of people interested in anthropomorphic animal characters. The subculture reached its zenith in mass culture with the help of the internet, allowing participants to connect and organise furry conventions such as Anthrocon, where fans can meet and engage in a range of fur-centric activities.

fursona
noun / portmanteau
Portmanteau of *furry* and *persona*; the character, alter ego, avatar, identity, or persona assumed by a member of the furry fandom community. (See also: **furry**, above.)

FWIW
initialism
For what it's worth.

FYEO
abbreviation / initialism
For your eyes only.

FYI
initialism
For your information. It can be used when attempting to elucidate a point but can also be employed when trying to add a little sass: *People don't actually call them 'jorts' anymore, FYI.*

fyre festival
noun
Meaning 'dumpster fire', this term is a reference to when, in 2017, a luxury music festival (Fyre Festival) ended in accusations of fraud and multi-million-dollar lawsuits.

G

gagged
verb
A feeling of amazement. To be 'gagged'
by something is to be 'blown away' or
'stunned'. The implication being that you
are so amazed by a person, event, or
speech that your breath has been taken
away. (See also: **shook**.)

gains
noun
Gains, and to 'make gains', is the
transformation of one's physique.
Making gains at the gym means
adding muscle mass and generally
getting fitter.

game recognise game
phrase
Acknowledging or recognising someone's
achievements and/or abilities. A proverbial
doffing of the hat.

game changer
noun
An event or element that significantly alters the outcome of something: *The addition of Sriracha to that mac and cheese was a total game changer.*

garbage fire
adjective
When a person is described as being 'garbage', it means they are worthless and despicable. A 'garbage fire' human is someone who encapsulates these negative traits, only the term dials 'garbage' up to 11. (See also: **dumpster fire**.)

gaslighting
verb
Gaslighting is a form of psychological manipulation and abuse in which the abuser tricks their victim into believing they are consistently wrong in their opinions and/or observations, resulting in the victim experiencing doubt and confusion. Online, this term has gained new relevancy and popularity.

gassed / gassed up

adjective

If one is 'gassed' or 'gassed up', then that person is brimming with self-confidence, sometimes to the point of either over-excitement or arrogance. This can be a term of derision, but depending on the context it can also be a neutral observation.

Generation Z

noun

The next generation after millennials, born sometime in the mid-1990s through to the 2000s. They probably know all the words in this book already. They grew up online, are tech savvy, and know their way around a social media account (or 30).

Germaneered

adjective

The most efficient way to state that something was engineered in Germany, which is kind of like German engineering in itself.

get that bread

phrase

To work hard for your money: *Off to work, finna get that bread!*

GF
initialism / noun
Short for *girlfriend*: *Me and the GF are ready for acroyoga this weekend!* (See also: **BF**.)

ghost / ghosting
verb
For a while this term meant leaving a party or event without bidding farewell to anyone. However, a more common usage now refers to dating, where a person never hears back from someone they were courting. *I don't know what happened. We had such a nice night. Then they just ghosted me...*

GIF
acronym / noun
Acronym for *Graphics Interchange Format,* one of the most common image formats online. (The inventor of the GIF, Steve Wilhite, continues to insist that, despite the first word of the acronym being *Graphics*, the correct pronunciation is *JIF*. The rest of the world continues to ignore him.)

giving me life
phrase
Energising, invigorating; something that is exciting, fun, uplifting, and making you feel good: *The latest season of* America's Next Top Candle Designer *is seriously giving me life.*

glamping
noun / portmanteau
Portmanteau of *glamourous* and *camping*; a style of camping that eschews the traditional goals of 'roughing it' and 'getting back to nature' in favour of bringing along all of the luxuries of home.

Globalian
noun
A member of the globe, which we all are; an entirely redundant name for a person who calls Earth their home.

glo up
verb
After one's awkward tween years, marred by puberty, some will 'glo up'. Which is to say they will, seemingly overnight, become really fucking attractive – they will 'glow'. (And yes, you must drop the 'w'!)

GMT

initialism

Meaning 'Getting Me Tight', or to 'get upset'.

GNOC

initialism

Get naked on camera. Our feeling is that if you're using this, then maybe don't? You shouldn't be using this.

GOAT

acronym / initialism

If someone or something is the GOAT, then they are the 'Greatest of All Time'.

Google doodle

noun

An altered, often interactive, version of the logo on Google's homepage; a temporary change designed to commemorate a person, event, or special day in the calendar.

goop

noun

Gwyneth Paltrow's wellness company... Yup, that's right. And you know this is a brand that stands for quality. (*Ahem.*)

gormazing
adjective
Portmanteau of *gorgeous* and *amazing*; an expression of pleasure, whether you're saying 'this food is wonderful' or 'that dress is lit'.

GPOY
initialism
Gratuitous picture of yourself.

grind
noun
Work, effort, slog, hustle; to be busy and doing your best: *Man, I am working 23-hour days, I am really on the grind.*

Grindr
noun
A social networking, dating, and hookup app specifically for queer people.

grip
noun
A lengthy period of time; while not an exact measurement, it does mean 'a lot': *I haven't been home in a grip; it took us a grip to finish that run; it's been a grip since I played* Mario Kart.

group chat
noun
A digital conversation among more than two people: *You know that feeling when your group chat is blowing up... magic.*

GTG
initialism
Good to go.

GTFO
initialism
Get the fuck out. This can be deployed as a legitimate request, or more humorously, as in: *GTFO... You did NOT just throw shade upon this outfit.*

Gucci
adjective
Talk about brand-name recognition... Gucci, in slang today, means 'good', 'doing well', 'fine', 'fresh', 'awesome', capitalising on the brand it originates from, a brand that stands for 'high end' or 'good quality'. In common parlance a response to the question *'How have you been?'* might be, *'Everything's been all Gucci.'*

gummies
noun
Traditionally meaning cannabinoid gummy bears, but which now extends to include any edible that resembles candy. Proceed with the utmost caution.

GYPO
initialism
Get your pants off. Like GNOC, maybe don't use this one?

H

H8
abbreviation
Hate.

HAK
initialism
Hugs and kisses.

hangry
adjective / portmanteau
When a person's hunger manifests as anger, they are hangry. This portmanteau describes the tantrums we're likely to enact when our blood-sugar levels drop. We've all been a cranky coworker, in the late afternoon, caught between lunch and dinner. That's hanger!

H

hashtag /
noun / prefix
The hash or pound symbol used to precede a word
or phrase, as part of a social media post. Primarily
used as a tag to assist search functionality, the
hashtag has since transcended its purpose and is now
used with expressive purpose to add context, depth,
or additional information, or to add a disclaimer.

haters
noun
Anybody (and we're waving our
metaphorical index finger in your face
as we tell you this), *anybody* who tries
to stand in your way. Easily identified by
their propensity to hate: *Haters gonna
hate, bro, just be yo'self, #YOLO*

HBIC
initialism
Head bitch in charge. The unquestionable
leader of a group/collective.

hella
adjective / adverb
Very, really; emphasises the degree to which something
is x or y. If something is *hella cool* then it's 'really
cool'. If something is *hella bad* then it is 'very bad'.

hells yeah
interjection
An incredibly obnoxious way of expressing your excitement in the affirmative: *'Wanna go fuck with some froyo?' 'Hells yeah!'*

heteronormative
adjective
Any attitude or point of view that takes or promotes heterosexuality as the 'normal' or given standard in regard to sexual orientation; a stance that does not assume alternative possibilities.

hey / heyyy / heyyyyyy
exclamation
While 'hey' remains an informal greeting, the number of y's attached to this word can change its subtext. Between two and four extra y's is generally a little flirty, while any more y's might mean the user is buttering you up for a favour: *Heyyyyyyy... so....*

hieee
exclamation
An alternative spelling for 'hello' or 'hi' or 'hey'. It remains a greeting, only all those extra e's just make it so much happier and fun. When said aloud, *hieee* must be high-pitched and protracted. (See also: **bieee**.)

HIFW
initialism
How I felt when.

high-key
adjective
When something is of great importance or is exceedingly obvious. This can refer to an extreme dislike or something positive that needs to be said. Either way, everybody needs to know. (See also: **low-key**.)

HMU
initialism
Hit me up. To get in touch or make contact with someone for a specific purpose; generally employed as a flirty invitation or with the implication of a booty call: *Hey babe, HMU when you get home!*

how it be
phrase
Another, and somehow more awful, way of saying *c'est la vie*. Used to express the hard facts of life or the state of the world: *'God, I can't even think about politics right now.'* *'I know, but that's just how it be.'*

HTH
initialism
Hope this helps.

humble brag
noun / verb
When a person wants to talk about themselves but lacks the temerity to do it outright, we end up with the 'humble brag' – self-praise buried under layers of false modesty. It's a frail attempt at humility, and everyone knows it!
I bought a $100,000 Tesla because climate change is just v important, you know?

hundo p
abbreviation
To be 100 percent sure about something: absolute certainty.
'You sure Billy's gonna show up tonight?'
'Hundo p, my man.'

hunty
portmanteau / verb
Portmanteau of *honey* and... well, something insulting beginning with 'c' they won't let me print here. An affectionate term from drag culture, recently popularised by the reality-television show *RuPaul's Drag Race*.

I

I see what you did there
phrase
Admiration for someone's wit, especially appropriate as an expression of approval with regard to a pun: *'Did you hear about the guy whose whole left side was cut off? He's all right now.' 'Oh. I see what you did there.'*

I'm just saying
phrase
Often employed to qualify an opinion, to make the opinion more subtle by obfuscation. The employment of the phrase is often redundant, as in: *'Wow, that movie sucked.' 'I really liked it.' 'Yeah, well, I'm just saying.'*

I'm baby
phrase
A catchall term of endearment, which may also express a desire for safety and comfort. This phrase has roots in dank meme culture but can be used in almost any context you wish, so feel free to use with total abandon.

ICAM
initialism
I couldn't agree more.

ICYMI
initialism
In case you missed it.

IDC
initialism
I don't care.

IDFWU
initialism
The initialism of *I don't fuck with you*, this phrase demonstrates not wanting anything to do with another person, generally due to animosity. Might be employed to signal the end of a relationship: *IDFWU anymore*.

IDGAF
acronym / initialism
I don't give a fuck.

IDK
initialism
I don't know.
Potential publisher: *So, what's your novel all about?*
Tobias: *IDK! Okay? I'm WORKING on it. Jeez.*

if you will
phrase
Commonly employed by people attempting to sound more intelligent and sophisticated than they actually are. Can be employed ironically, too: *You could say, if you will, that I'm 'in the biz', if you will.*

IFYP
initialism
I feel your pain.

IKR
initialism
I know, right?

immersive design
noun
Online content, video games, and web designs that provide users with an 'immersive' experience, meaning that the users feel engaged and stimulated by the content or program they are using.

impact
noun
Effect, influence: *The work of James Joyce has had a big impact on my career as an author.*

IMO / IMHO
initialism
Meaning *in my opinion / in my humble opinion*, these qualifiers are used to preface a sentence that is clearly an opinion, making it redundant: *IMHO, Jerry Seinfeld's career-defining performance was in* Bee Movie.

IMU
initialism
I miss you.

incel
noun / portmanteau
Hybridising the words 'involuntary' and 'celibate', an incel is someone whose inability to find a romantic or sexual partner defines their existence, and often, in their own mind, typifies the 'oppression' of men in the twenty-first century. Simply put: *yiiiikes*.

influencer
noun
Someone who influences others. Today, this is most commonly ascribed to 'tastemakers' on social media platforms like Instagram. Beware, there are many people who think they're influencers, who really ain't...

Instaworthy
adjective
Denoting that something is incredibly visually appealing and also notable, thus worthy of posting to Instagram: *You look gormazing in that dress. Totes Instaworthy.*

IOW
initialism
In other words.

IRL
initialism
In real life. In an era when so much of our lives play out online, sometimes you have to make the distinction!

irregardless
adverb
Regardless. *Irregardless* is not a real word; the combination of prefix *ir–* and suffix *–less* work to cancel each other out, meaning that those who employ this term technically say the opposite of what they mean to say.

it me
phrase
Used when a person relates strongly with something being expressed by another, whether an image or a quote or something being said. For example: You see that someone has posted a picture of their pug snorting happily, and because you're also feeling contented, you might comment *'it me'*.

it's a thing
phrase
Used to dispel incredulity regarding whether or not something is, in fact, a 'thing': *Vegan fried chicken? Yeah. It's a thing*, or, *'Men's Rights Activists? Are you fucking kidding me?' 'I know... It's a thing.'*

it's been real
phrase
Signalling the end. Usually used as a farewell before a departure and generally denoting a good experience has been had by the user: *Thanks for standing in for my girlfriend today. It's been real.*

it's complicated
phrase
Conveys that a subject is not open for further discussion; usually used in context with regard to personal matters: *'How are things going between you and Sam after the Vaseline incident?' 'It's complicated...'*

ITT
initialism
In this thread.

IWSN
initialism
I want sex now. Okay, well... fair enough?

J

jackintosh
noun / portmanteau
Portmanteau of *Macintosh* (the original Apple desktop computer) and *jack off* (meaning, to masturbate): a computer used exclusively for viewing pornography.

jelly
abbreviation / adjective
Short for *jealous*: *Tanya is so jelly of Sid, whose new BF is totes hot AF.*

JFDI
abbreviation / initialism
Initialism of *just fucking do it*; the classic Nike slogan with some added punch. If you're ever in need of motivation, just remind yourself: *JFDI.*

JK
initialism
Short for *just kidding*; sometimes employed accompanying text in digital conversation where, due to the absence of tone and inflection, the intention of what is being said may not be clear to the recipient: *Eugh, I just wish you would die. JK!*

JOMO
acronym / noun
The antonym of FOMO, JOMO means the 'Joy of Missing Out'. It refers to the pleasure of staying in the present moment, the joy to be had in ignoring your social media accounts and not worrying what's happening in the rest of the world. Sometimes it's just really healthy to miss out, and to not care.

JSYK
initialism
Just so you know.

JTLYK
initialism
Just to let you know.

J

Juggalo

noun

A fan of American hip-hop duo Insane Clown Posse (ICP), a rap group comprised of two literal clowns known as Violent J and Shaggy 2 Dope. Together the ICP perform a style of hardcore hip-hop music known as 'horrorcore'. These fans dress in terrifying clown attire and are known for being cult-like and obsessive.

juul

noun

A very slim 'vape', which just about anyone can get their hands on. Good to know your kids can smoke in schools again... Although it might look like they're suckling a USB stick.

K

keep it
phrase / verb
Indicates approval: *Honey, your crop top is bomb. Keep it.*

keep it 100
phrase / verb
To be true to yourself and to others, to always be 100 percent sincere in your actions and words. Akin to the phrase 'keep it real'.

KFY
initialism
Kiss for you. Mostly used as a signoff: *See you tomorrow, sweetie. KFU!*

kiki
noun / verb
This is a word used for gossip, small talk, or heart-to-heart conversations.

K

killed it
phrase / verb
To have unambiguously succeeded.

KMN
initialism
Kill me now. Just to be on the safe side, add JK!

kombucha
noun
Fermented, lightly effervescent, sweetened tea drink known for its alleged probiotic health benefits. Brewed by hipsters who subscribe to notions of 'wellness', often made in jars full of murky brown liquid and topped with bacterial sludge.

KOTL
initialism
Kiss on the lips.

KPC
initialism
Keeping parents clueless.

K-pop

abbreviation / noun

K-pop is a music genre from South Korea that is hugely popular around the world. The flourishing successor to J-pop (Japanese pop), K-pop draws upon many genres, including traditional folk. But what defines K-pop is the intense fandom surrounding its 'idol' groups.

kthxbai

abbreviation / phrase

Okay, thanks, bye. This is your all-in-one abbreviation, a quick and convenient signoff for many occasions.

L

LB
initialism
Short for 'like back', this term is employed on social media between users looking to up their likes. If I like your something, then you should like my something, too. It's only fair, right?

left on read
phrase
To be 'left on read' means that your text message, for example, has been seen by the recipient but they have not responded. To be 'left on read' is an insult of the highest order and can lead to feelings of dejection as a result of such damning neglect.

legit
abbreviation / adjective
Abbreviation of *legitimate*; valid, sound, or well founded. Formally reserved for absolutes, this can also be employed as a statement of opinion: *OMFG, this burger is so legit.*

let my girls hang
phrase
Not wearing a bra; generally associated with the sweet relief of removing your bra: *I can't wait to get home and let my girls hang.*

levelution
noun / portmanteau
Portmanteau of *level* and *evolution;* the process of increasing in popularity. As someone or something becomes more famous or popular, they progressively level up: *In recent years, movie-goers have witnessed the levelution of actor Margot Robbie.*

life
noun
Amazing, the most incredible thing in your existence at the present time: *Duuuuude, this chocolate cake is life.* (See also: **giving me life.**)

life admin
noun
Personal administrative tasks, such as emailing, banking, and paying bills, and making a schedule for various upcoming events, including booking appointments. Basically, chores for adults.

life changing
phrase
Any experience or event that elicits extreme emotions: *That seminar was life changing*.

life hack
noun
A shortcut or work-around; a tool, system, or idea that you can employ to make a task simpler. Life hacks might include using a grapefruit and salt to polish glass, paying someone to queue for you when you don't have the time to wait, and blowing into your game cartridge when your Nintendo 64 won't load properly.

like
conjunction
Employed as a way to stall for emphasis; an in-sentence pause. Can also be used deliberately and/or ironically: *We were all just, like, hanging out until, like, Mark came along and just, like, went batshit for, like, no reason at all.* Or: *Like, hello? Are you, like, stupid or something?*

listicle

noun / portmanteau

Portmanteau of *list* and *article*; an article presented in the form of a list. The headlines of these articles usually include the number of items in the list, such as, '16 Olympians Who Are Really, Really Ridiculously Good Looking' or '73 Acid-Wash Jumpsuits You Need This Christmas'.

lit

adjective

Awesome, excellent, unparalleled; used when you need to express how great something is. Can also mean that something has 'popped off', or that someone is drunk, especially if their behaviour is outlandish: *I heard that party the other week was lit.* Or: *Check this guy out! Guillermo is lit!*

literally

adverb

Figuratively. Yes, this words now means the opposite of what it, literally, means. An amplifier used to emphasis the impact of information, especially when the statement is clearly exaggerated: *My iPhone is literally my best friend and lover.*

live
adjective
Exciting, cool, awesome, amazing; can also imply that this same thing was intense or extreme in some way: *'How was Jayden's fondue party last night?' 'Oh, man, it was seriously live.'*

LMAO
abbreviation / acronym / initialism
Laughing my ass off. You might want to try simply using an emoji in place of this acronym, as it's a bit... 2009. But it's difficult to otherwise convey one's ass coming off.

LMFAO
initialism
Laughing my fucking ass off. You know, for when LMAO just isn't getting it done...

LMK
initialism
Let me know; do confide when the information is readily available.

LOL
acronym / initialism / verb
Laugh out loud. The most ubiquitous three letters in twenty-first century communication. You already know what this means. (We hope.)

lols / lulz
noun
Fun, laughter, amusement; originating from LOL, meaning laughing out loud.

lose-lose
noun / phrase
A scenario whereby, no matter what occurs, the outcome will be negative. Generally, this implies that you have to make a choice between two or more options, and all choices will lead to a negative result. (See also: **win-win**.)

low-key
adjective / phrase
Used to describe casual soirees and get togethers, which would preferably remain between a small group of close friends. Also used to mean 'subtly' or 'somewhat', as in: *He's giving me, like, low-key fuckboi vibes... Right?* (See also: **high-key**.)

M

M8
abbreviation / noun
Shorthand for 'mate'. Commonly in territories where mate is used as a term of endearment, or as a synonym for 'friend', such as in the UK, Ireland, Australia, and New Zealand.

mansplaining
portmanteau / verb
Portmanteau of *man* and *explaining*; the act of men speaking in a condescending manner to others (typically, a woman) with the invalid assumption that he knows more about the subject at hand than the person he is talking to: *My dad totally mansplained intersectional feminism to me last night.*

manspreading
verb
The action of a man taking up a large amount of space in a shared or public area (often, public transport), by sitting with legs spread wide apart, with no regard to the inconvenience and discomfort caused to those beside him.

Marie Kondo
noun / verb
The process of removing needless items in the home, based on a set of strict criteria – namely whether or not the object 'sparks joy' within you. The principle was established by author Marie Kondo in her bestselling self-help guide *The Life-Changing Magic of Tidying Up*, and her subsequent Netflix series.

marketability
noun
The degree to which something is able to be marketed towards a general audience or specific demographic: *We were going to put Lindsay Lohan in our ad campaign, but she's got no marketability anymore.*

Marvel Cinematic Universe / MCU
noun
A cinematic franchise of films produced by Marvel Studios, based on Marvel comics, all set in the same fictional universe. Movies within the MCU include *Iron Man*, *Thor*, *Captain America*, and *The Avengers*.

megaphone
noun
The jerk talking too loudly on their phone, in public: *He just won't shut up! Christ, what a megaphone douche.*

meh
adjective / interjection
A verbal shrug; expresses indifference.
Can be used as a response to a question:
'What did you think of Thor 17*?' 'Meh.'* Or
as description: *I liked the performances
in* Monopoly: The Movie, *but the
costumes were kind of meh.*

meme
noun
An image, video, or piece of text, usually
comic in nature, that is copied and spread
rapidly by internet users.

memephobia
noun
The fear that something will go viral, just like a meme;
a concern that a picture or footage of you, in a
compromising or humiliating situation, may find a global
audience and bring you unwanted fame. (See also: **viral**.)

MFW
initialism
My face when: *MFW Tina did that
quadruple backflip.*

mic drop
verb / phrase
The metaphoric or figurative act of dropping a microphone after delivering an amazing performance, where this action serves to punctuate said performance. One may feign the act of dropping a microphone, or just say '*mic drop*' before leaving the conversation or stage.

millennial
noun
A person who reached a stage of adolescence or young adulthood around the year 2000; also known as generation Y. There is no official demarcation of the much-derided millennial generation, but it is generally thought to be those born between the early 1980s and mid-1990s.

mindfulness
noun
A state of heightened self-awareness. It's all about focusing on the present moment! This term's prevalence now suggests a kind of backlash to (or a mindfulness of) the way we're leading our lives, so immersed in technology as we are. (See also: **digital detox**.)

M

'mirin
abbreviation / verb
Short for *admiring*; often written without the apostrophe simply as *mirin*: *Hey, baby, you mirin me? Because I can see you lookin'.*

MIRL
initialism
Me in real life. You know, as opposed to ZIRL (zebras in real life) or NIRL (newts in real life). And not to be confused, of course, with giraffes in real life or manta rays in real life or bubble tea in real life...

MMW
initialism
Mark my words.

moblivious
adjective / portmanteau
Portmanteau of *mobile* and *oblivious*; lack of awareness that results from staring at a mobile phone screen: *Those damn pesky kids not looking where they're going are completely moblivious to their surroundings!* (See also: **phubbing**.)

M

mom / mum
noun
Much in the same way 'dad' can refer to a person's positive traits, 'mom' or 'mum' (depending on where you're from) is a stand-in for someone who demonstrates responsibility. The mom/mum of any group (or *squad*) is the most responsible member.

mood
noun
The new word for 'same', 'mood' is an affirmative catchall used to express agreement or when something posited is relatable and/or correct. What you say when you understand the sentiment.
Carol: *'Went on another bad Tinder date last night. No love.'*
Greg: *'Mood.'*

MRW
initialism
My reaction when.

mug
noun
A person's face. Mug is an old word (*look at that ugly mug*) that has seen recent revival, particularly in drag culture: *She's so good at beating her mug.* (See also: **beat face.**)

mukbang
noun
A video of someone eating; specifically, a form popularised in South Korea during the early 2010s, whereby a 'host' eats large quantities of food while interacting with their audience via chatrooms.

MVP
initialism / noun
Initialism of *most valuable player*; traditionally used in a sporting context, whereby awards given at the end of a season may include the MVP trophy. However, MVP can also refer to someone whose work or contribution or personality you deem super valuable.

Mx
pronoun
A gender neutral and/or queer formal pronoun that replaces other formal pronouns such as Ms, Mrs, or Mr.

MYOB
initialism
Mind your own business. Sage advice!

nailed it
phrase / verb
To unequivocally succeed at something; to get a flawless result. Can be employed ironically to mean the opposite, indicating a humorous failure: *My rainbow cupcakes came out looking like lumpy brown potatoes. Nailed it.*

NC
abbreviation / initialism
No comment.

neg
noun / verb
A negative comment primarily intended to make someone feel bad, but most commonly employed as a pick-up technique that deliberately undermines confidence in a way that makes a person more receptive to advances. This action is referred to as *negging*.

nerdgasm
noun / portmanteau
Portmanteau of *nerd* and *orgasm*; the extreme excitement expressed by a nerd over something nerdy: *When Jason watched* The Flash *for the first time, he had a nerdgasm over how fast that dude could run.*

Netflix and chill
phrase / verb2
The act of relaxing and watching programs via streaming services, like Netflix, often with company. Also used in online-dating circles as a euphemism for a hookup: *Hey, you down to Netflix and chill?*

New phone who dis?
phrase
A commonly asked phrase after receiving a text or missed call from an unknown number. The brilliance of this tactic, of course, is you that don't even need to have a new phone to ask it.

newsjacking
portmanteau / verb
Portmanteau of *news* and *hijacking*; exploiting a breaking-news story in order to advertise or to promote a brand or product. Harnessed maliciously in 2016 to elect a nincompoop to the highest office of the USA.

next level
phrase
Elevated in quality. If the burger you just ate or the song you recently heard is *next level* then that burger or that song is, respectively, a better burger or song than the majority of other burgers or songs: *Have you heard Kendrick's new record? That is some next level shit*.

NIFOC
initialism
Naked in front of computer,,, umm... so...

NIMBY
acronym
Not in my backyard. An exclusionist, xenophobic catch cry, used by certain nationalist groups.

NM
initialism
There are two possible meanings here, depending on context: *never mind* or *nothing much*.

N

NNTR
initialism
No need to reply. No seriously, *NNTR*.

nocialise
portmanteau / verb
Portmanteau of *no* and *socialise*. Any anti-social behaviour brought about by the use of technology, such as ignoring people in favour of playing games on your mobile device. (See also: **phubbing**.)

noob / n00b
abbreviation / noun
Meaning 'newbie': someone who is new to something. Usually carrying connotations of naivety.

normcore
noun / adjective
A fashion style characterised by the elevation of bland, dad-like, or otherwise 'normal' clothing, with the intention of positioning the wearer as conspicuously unpretentious. The very fact of its existence and its (ambiguously ironic) popularity with hipsters has turned the style into a trend, making its claim of being unpretentious decidedly pretentious.

normie

noun

A 'normie' is someone who is so 'normal' they're boring, almost pathetic. It's a lot like describing someone as 'basic', only 'normie' is often a statement of fact, rather than an insult.

NOYB

initialism

None of your business.

NP

initialism

No problem. A great catchall for patching up with friends or for expressing the ease with which the request of a favour is received.

NSFL

initialism

Not safe for life. (See also: **NSFW**. Only, more so...)

NSFW
initialism
Initialism of *not safe for work*. Used in a link or an email subject line to warn that 'adult' content lies within, therefore being something you won't want displayed on your computer screen should your manager happen to walk past.

NTIM
initialism
Not that it matters.

nudes
abbreviation / noun
Shorthand for 'nude photographs', this is language found in any typical sext transcript. A commonplace request in the world of online dating might also be to 'send nudes'.

'nuff said
phrase
Short *for enough said*; a full stop of sorts, saying 'you needn't say anymore' and 'message received': *Michael Jordan was the greatest basketball player to ever hit the court. 'Nuff said.*

OATUS
acronym / initialism
On a totally unrelated subject. This makes for a nice, albeit abrupt, segue... It also looks and sounds like something bodyguards might call the person they've been paid to protect.

obvi
adjective
Short for *obvious* or *obviously*; reached popularity through the hit teen drama show *The O.C.* back in the mid-2000s. And, of late, it is making a quasi-ironic resurgence. *Obvi* is best served with a side of eye roll. Those who want to get their sass on need only employ this word in place of 'duh'.

OG
initialism / noun
Initialism of *original gangster*. The term has found broad use as a synonym for 'original', with nostalgic connotations: *Paris Hilton was totally the OG reality queen. Kim Kardashian would be nothing if it weren't for Paris.* (See also: **old school**.)

OIC
initialism
Oh, I see!

old school
adjective
Old fashioned, but often used with an implication of respect and deference. If someone is described as being old school, then they conjure sensibilities associated with past eras: *That gramophone is seriously old school. Where's the aux cord, bruh?*

OMG
initialism
Oh my god! You knew this one already, didn't you? *OMG*, please tell us you knew this one already!

OMFG
initialism
Oh my fucking god! Look, sometimes OMG just isn't getting it across right...

OMW
initialism
On my way.

O

on blast
phrase
To draw attention to a person or thing in a critical manner: *Sorry, Diane, but I'm going to have to put you on blast right now. That was totally NOT cool.*

on point
adjective
Perfection, exactness, highly suitable; used to state that something is of excellent quality: *Oh yeah, that joint's pizza game is on point.*

OP
initialism
Original post. Used in forums to refer readers back to the very first post, the reason we're all here.

or nah?
phrase
At the end of a sentence, this phrase can be used as a clarification, when you require a concrete answer: *Are you going to that party tonight, or nah?*

O

origin story
noun
How a person or thing came to be in the present moment. Most commonly used in reference to comic books and films, especially with regard to superheroes, the origin story can often be an interesting piece of history, or a worn-out reboot of something we've all heard before: *Everyone knows Batman's mother and father were murdered in the alley. Move on already!*

ORLY
abbreviation
Oh, really?

OT
initialism
Off topic.

othering
verb
The marginalising of a person, or group of people, in a way that positions them as different to a presumed 'normal'; to make a person feel alien and/or to treat them as such.

O

OTL
initialism
Out to lunch. How... wholesome.

OTOH
initialism
On the other hand.

OTP
initialism
Initialism of *one true pairing*; refers to a couple whose relationship you are emotionally invested in, whose break-up would pain you. This couple may be people you know personally, but most commonly your OTP are a celebrity couple you've never met, and the phrase is meant semi-ironically. Your OTP might be Kanye and Kim, or, more likely, Beyoncé and Jay-Z.

OTT
initialism
Over the top. When somebody takes things just a little too far. Or, perhaps, way too fucking far.

O

own
verb
To dominate; to aggressively and decisively take victory over something or someone. Alternatively, it can be used inversely to describe someone or something *getting owned: Taylor Swift got completely owned by Kim and Kanye.* Or: *'How did you go with your pitch?' 'I totally owned it!'*

oxygen thief
noun
A person so worthless that the purpose of their existence seems solely to deprive those around them of vital oxygen.

P

p
abbreviation
Why write entire words when we can just use the first letter? P, in this case, stands for 'pretty': as in 'p cool', meaning 'pretty cool'.

PAL
acronym / initialism
No, not your friend or your buddy, *PAL* stands for *parents are listening*.

pan / pansexual
adjective / noun
A person whose sexual orientation is non-specific and not limited; attracted to people of any sex or gender.

paper
noun
Straight-up cash: *I'm heading into work, because I gotta make that paper.* (See also: **bread**.)

parkour
noun
Also known as *free running*, a form of movement that reimagines urban spaces so that practitioners can navigate their environment, without assistive equipment, in the most efficient and fastest way possible. A training discipline and form of exercise that originated in France in the 1980s. While utterly impractical, parkour does look pretty damn cool.

PAW
abbreviation / acronym / initialism
Initialism of *parents are watching*; a warning to whoever you are chatting with, letting them know that your parents are around and that you might be being monitored, therefore the tone and content need to stay 'parent friendly'. (See also: **NSFW**.)

peacocking
verb
When a human being dresses flamboyantly in order to draw attention from a desired sexual partner, just like a peacock displaying its vibrant plumage.

PEBKAC
acronym / initialism
Problem exists between keyboard and chair. This is any IT professional's way of kindly saying that the issues being uncovered are not technical ones, but the fault of the user having no idea what they are doing.

peeps
abbreviation / noun
Short for *people*; commonly used in the possessive context to indicate a group you might be affiliated with, whether it be your family, your friends, a sports team or social-interest group. *I'm catching up with my Hufflepuff peeps later. Gonna learn how to make butterbeer.*

photobomb
verb
The act of intruding in a photograph, usually by deliberately disrupting the picture being taken or by standing in the background. While the intention is generally to spoil the outcome, if a cute animal should inadvertently *photobomb* you, then the resulting image will be internet gold.

phubbing
portmanteau / verb
Portmanteau of *phone* and *snub*; to ignore your companion(s) and instead direct your attention towards your phone.

PIR
initialism
Parents in room.

PITA
abbreviation / acronym / initialism
Pain in the ass.

plug
verb
Meaning 'to promote': *You check Twitter today? Everyone's been plugging Oprah's new book.*

PLZ
abbreviation / acronym
Please.

PMFI

initialism

Pardon me for interrupting. This one sounds a little snarky, doesn't it? *Well, PMFI...*

POC

initialism

Short for 'person of colour' or 'people of colour'.

portmanNO

noun / portmanteau

A modern portmanteau word that you find so particularly idiotic and intellectually offensive that you literally can't even. This dictionary is filled with *portmanNOs*, including *phubbing, listicle,* and *nocialise.*

POS

acronym / initialism

Another initialism designed to prevent snooping, POS can mean *parent over shoulder.* It might also stand for piece of shit: *My car is a total POS.* But for the people working in retail and hospitality out there, then you know the abbreviation as point of sale!

P

post
noun
Publication of material online; an upload of content to the internet, commonly associated with blogs or social media: *Have you seen Sharon's latest post? Like, Sharon, we GET IT: you have a baby.*

POV
initialism
Point of view.

power couple
noun
A couple of two powerful individuals, where that power can be economic, cultural, political, intellectual, or otherwise: *Beyoncé and Jay Z are music's greatest power couple.*

preach
interjection
An encouraging affirmation: *'Oprah Winfrey is a goddamn national treasure.' 'Preach!'*

problematic

adjective

Instead of simply suggesting that a problem has been presented, *problematic* now often suggests a perceived ethical dilemma regarding a person, institution, word, phrase, event, image, and so on. For example: *X is so problematic... Because his lyrics are clearly misogynist garbage. But, fuck, that track is lit.*

procrastibation

noun / portmanteau

The art of avoiding certain deadlines or chores by, well, masturbating. It's a kind of procrastination that's as old as humankind.

q-gasm
noun
An orgasm experienced after sticking a Q-tip into your ear. Yup...

QFT
initialism
Quoted for truth; commonly used on internet forums where its employment is used to, generally, agree with another forum user.

QPOC
initialism
QPOC stands for 'queer person of colour' or 'queer people of colour'.

QT
abbreviation / noun
Short for cutie: *What up, QT?*

queen bee
noun
An 'alpha' or 'leader of the pack'. Usually a term reserved for high schoolers: *The queen bee showed up late to the party, in order to make an apt entrance.*

question fart
noun
Passing wind where the sound ends in an upward inflection, similar to the inflection you would use when asking a question.

quickie
noun
Sexual intercourse performed in a timely manner.

quirper
noun
A creepy, creepy human who derives sexual pleasure from sniffing bicycle seats.

ratchet
adjective
Alternate spelling of *wretched*; originally a derogatory term for a person perceived as obnoxious and trashy, but which now has a broader use, describing anything broken or dysfunctional: *My chain came off, this bike is ratchet!*

reach out
verb
To make contact by any available means; the phrase has grandiose connotations, as though the person making contact believes they are doing you an enormous favour by bestowing their attention on you: *I had to reach out to William to discuss what he's wearing to my party, so I gave him a call.*

read
verb
To point out someone's flaws in a sassy, witty, and accurate manner; can be delivered in a humorous manner, similar to that of a roast. A comedic critique.

reality check
noun
Employed with the intention of bringing a person into the life of those around them, to ground them or to bring them back to 'reality'. *'So, I'm thinking about becoming an astronaut.' 'Ummm. Quick reality check... I think you need to know about, like, physics and stuff.'*

realness
noun / adjective
A quick way of referring to anything that might be deemed 'the real deal', meaning genuine and/or great. Also, mostly in drag culture, realness can qualify the accuracy and precision of the look being served: *Darling, this outfit is giving me misanthropic venture-capitalist realness.*

reboot
verb / noun
Most commonly used in relation to the resurrection of a dormant Hollywood film property or franchise, whereby the original film is remade with a different cast, as opposed to continuing the story with a sequel.

receipts
noun
In the current social landscape in which many celebrities have been called out for past actions, 'receipts' refer to the evidence gathered of any person's past transgressions and of their general hypocrisy. In this context, 'receipts' are generally screenshots of past social media, instant messaging, or email correspondences: *Don't you dare come for me. You better believe I kept the receipts!*

rekt
verb
Alternative spelling of *wrecked*; something or someone who has in some way been hurt or humiliated: *Jeremy tried parkour, but then she face-planted and totally rekt herself.*

relatability
noun
The degree to which something is or is not relatable, either to a mass audience or specific demographic. A person's *relatability* is their ability for others to identify with them.

repost
noun / verb
Something that commonly occurs on message boards and social media platforms. To repost something is to post a link to a story or item of interest that has already been posted and discussed. On message boards, a repost is a serious *faux pas*.

resonate
verb
To evoke a shared feeling; usually the way an event, subject, or persona is accepted by an audience. Essentially, resonate has come to replace the word 'relate'. If someone or something resonates with others, then it 'goes over well': *Actor Chris Pratt really resonates with the 18–25-year-old demographic.*

respek
noun
Respect; to give something the respect it deserves and/or is due. When you put *respek* on someone's names you draw attention to them in a positive way.

responsive web design
noun
Code that allows websites to adapt the way it displays depending on the size of window and type of device it's viewed on. Increasingly, a standard of web design.

retrogaming
verb
Sometimes called 'classic gaming' or 'old school gaming', *retrogaming* is playing old games on old consoles. The one qualification for a 'retrogame' is that the system you're playing on has been discontinued or is obsolete. If you're still holding regular *GoldenEye 007* tournaments, then you have the geeky heart of a retrogamer.

rich media
noun
A term used to describe interactive elements of web design, usually used to refer to advertising such as a banner advert on a website that expands when you click on it, or the Google doodle.

ridic
abbreviation / adjective
Short for 'ridiculous': *He looked ridic in that bowler hat, OMFG*

RLY
abbreviation
Really.

RN
initialism
Right now.

RT
abbreviation / verb
Short for *retweet*, which is a function of Twitter, whereby you share someone else's post with your own followers.

RU
initialism
Are you?

R

rude
exclamation
A handy retort for when something isn't going one's way. Used contemporarily as a synonym for *WTF?* For example: *Umm, Jerry won't reply to my email, but he's out here liking my Instagram post?? Rude.*

RUOK?
initialism
Are you okay? For something seemingly so genuine, reducing this sentiment to an abbreviation kind of takes the wind out of its sails now, doesn't it?

RYS
initialism
Are you single? Maybe the three least appealing words in the English language... Well, it all depends on who's asking...

S

sadiculous
adjective / portmanteau
Portmanteau of *sad* and *ridiculous*; conveys that something is very sad – ridiculously so. This word is generally employed where the meaning of sad is closer to pathetic: *He was trying so hard to dance like Backpack Kid, it was unbelievably sadiculous.*

safe space
noun
A place where someone feels safe from harassment. While the term once talked about literal 'spaces', this now often means any friendly and/or inclusive environment: *Feel free to vent, you're in a safe space.*

salty
adjective
Irritated, angry: *After lining up for four hours and missing out on the last cronut, I'm a little salty right now.*

sarcaustic
adjective / portmanteau
Portmanteau of *sarcastic* and *caustic*; a tone of scathing irony used to convey contempt.

savage
adjective / verb
Biting but in a cheeky way, so as to not be able to tell whether or not one is being serious: *RuPaul is such a savage, she throws the best shade.*

SCNR
initialism
Sorry, could not resist. Depending on what the user could not resist, this could be endearing or all-out terrifying.

screen rage
noun
Anger that is directed at a screen. If you've ever blown up at your iPhone while scrolling through your news app, especially during the election coverage, then you've experienced *screen rage*.

self-care
noun
That act of taking care of one's own self, generally with regard to a person's long-term wellbeing. It highlights one's physical and *mental* health as matters of great importance, and justifies the price tag of semi-regular designer facemasks.

selfie
noun
A photograph of yourself, taken by... yourself.

SEP
initialism
Someone else's problem. If you find yourself using this acronym, it might be time to reevaluate some things about yourself...

seriously
adverb
An indicator that you mean something in earnest: *I am seriously dying to get out of this room. Seriously, it's seriously hot in here.*

sext
noun / verb
A text message of a sexually explicit nature; can be a text, or a photograph. *Sext* can refer to the message itself, or the act of sending the message: *We've been sexting for about a month now. I think they might be THE ONE.*

SFLR
initialism
Sorry for late reply. This is a handy one to get yourself familiar with, as it covers for an all-too-common problem when we're inundated with blips and beeps and buzzes from our phones.

shade / throwing shade
noun / verb
'Shade' is an insult, or a backhanded compliment, which demonstrates fierce wit and sass. This is bitchiness personified! But bitchiness that's too clever and enjoyable to take to heart.

sharing economy
noun
An economic system in which assets or services are shared between private individuals either for free or for a fee, typically facilitated by the internet. Companies such as Airbnb and Uber are based on this mode.

ship
abbreviation / verb
Short for *relationship*; the projected desire for a relationship to occur between two people, fictional or otherwise. Employed by fans of the two people who want to see them together: *I'm shipping the living shit out of Timothée Chalamet and Armie Hammer.*

shitshow
noun
An event or moment in time when things go to... well, *shit*. A disaster. Chaos. A real *shitshow*! (See also: **clusterfuck**.)

shook
adjective
To be 'shook' is to be in a state of utter disbelief and/or confusion. This word derives from the phrase 'to be shaken up' by something: *And, it turns out, the bagel had been sitting there for three days. I was shook.*

shooketh
adjective
When 'shook' isn't enough to describe your state of disbelief, you are beyond shook, you are shooketh. For example: *And, it turns out, the bagel had been sitting there for three fucking YEARS. I am shooketh to my very core.*

shots fired
phrase
Referencing the military tactic of firing warning shots, 'shots fired' is used to suggest that a disagreement is about to really heat the fuck up!
Jason: *He's just saying that because he knows he'll never work in this industry again.*
Sarah: *OoOOOooOOoooh, shots fired!*

shoutout
noun / verb
A public acknowledgement; to mention someone publicly in a positive manner.

shut it down
phrase / verb
Meaning 'put an end to' something – a call for an event or moment to stop, to cease. For example: Your friend is getting a bit too rowdy at your party and so you call for them to '*Shut it down!*'

sickening
adjective
Causing a level of discomfort, due to overwhelming levels of something typically perceived as positive: *God, Jonathan Van Ness's outfit is simply sickening. I literally can't even.*

side hustle
noun
A secondary source of income. That weekend hobby, which now has you selling ceramics at the arts market – it's nothing like your day job, but it brings in a little cash on the side.

siriris
acronym / noun
Alternative term for *palindrome*; also an acronym for *spelled in reverse it remarkably is same*. Has the advantage over a palindrome in that it demonstrates the quality it describes; has the disadvantage of being a bit stupid and annoying.

sis
abbreviation / noun
Short for *sister*; can describe your biological sister, but it is more commonly employed to describe a member of your squad; your bestie, your homie, the person you take all those selfies with. (See also: **BFF**.)

SITD
initialism
Still in the dark. Whatever you do, don't forget the 'I'…

skrrt
interjection / onomatopoeia
The sound of car wheels screeching has become a slang response for any situation one wants to get away from, and quickly. The next time you're in an awkward situation, say '*skrrrrrt*', then bounce. Works like a charm.

SLAP
acronym / initialism
Sounds like a plan. Not to be confused with the act of hitting someone...

slaps
verb
When something 'slaps' then it's truly great. It's often used to describe music, particularly any song with a tantalising bassline or hook: *Damn this track fucking slaps!*

slay
verb
To succeed, in a way that suggests any competitors have been annihilated; to dominate: *I think we can agree that Beyoncé slays harder than any of y'all.*

slide into your DMs
phrase
To 'slide into' one's DMs is the act of directly messaging someone on social media. Usually this would be someone you have never met, or someone with whom you're only vaguely acquainted. Sliding into DMs is the quintessential form of flirting in the twenty-first century.

smash
verb
This is increasingly millennial's and xennial's euphemism of choice for referring to the act of sex. To *smash*.

SMH
initialism
Initialism of shaking my head, SMH is an abbreviation used to convey that the user finds something so stupid that they are lost for words: *'I've never been concussed, so I deliberately smashed my head against a wall to see what it feels like.'* 'What happened?' 'Nothing. I just have a headache' 'SMH.'

smize
noun / verb
To smile using only your eyes; a modelling technique coined by supermodel and creator/presenter of *America's Next Top Model,* Tyra Banks.

snatched
adjective
Flawless, on point. If your outfit is tight, it's *snatched*. If you're slayin' in your cocktail dress, you're *snatched*.

sneaker head
noun
A sneaker obsessive! What else? A sneaker head is someone who owns way too many pairs of Yeezys and/or is an avid collector.

SO
abbreviation / initialism
Significant other. A great catchall term for boyfriends, girlfriends, partners, husbands, wives, and lovers. Best of all: it's gender neutral.

social justice warrior / SJW
noun
A combative personality whose cries for social justice are perceived as annoying and deliberately antagonistic (and thus, often ineffectual). Typically, a *SJW*'s primary means of enacting societal change is by hurling abuse at strangers on Twitter.

sorry, not sorry

phrase

Indicates that you are sorry that someone disagrees, but that you will happily ignore the difference in opinion and proceed as intended. A linguistic shrug of the shoulders.

soy boy

noun

A pejorative term for a man who eschews archaic traits of masculinity. *Soy boy* takes its name from the consumption of *bougie* soy products, like soy lattes, which some have (misleadingly) claimed have diminishing effects on the male libido.

spollers

noun

A statement that must accompany any review or comment regarding a movie, TV show, or video game, warning the reader/viewer/listener that plot points are going to be revealed. Failure to do so, and the subsequent 'spoiling' that occurs, will bring the wrath of the entire internet down upon your head.

squad

noun

Your crew or posse. In plain English, it means 'a group of friends'.

squad goals
noun
If your 'squad' is your group or friendship circle, then 'squad goals' are the achievements or aspirational ideals one intends for their social group.

SRSLY?
abbreviation
Seriously? *Is it worth it to you to drop those few extra letters? SRSLY?*

SRY
abbreviation
Sorry. (See joke above.)

stan
noun / portmanteau / verb
Portmanteau of *stalker* and *fan*, this term was popularised by the Eminem song 'Stan' in 2000. Since then, a *stan* has been anyone who takes their fandom to an obsessive level. But today, *stan* is used as a verb, conveying more general fandom: *We stan Beyoncé's new track!* Or: *OMG. The new Beyoncé track??? I stan.*

standard

adjective / noun

The natural order of things; anything that is to be assumed or expected, or that which goes without saying. For example: When a hard-partying friend turns up to your causal dinner party with an entire beer keg, you might fold your arms, smirk, and declare that this is *standard*.

starchitect

noun

Portmanteau of *star* and *architect*; any world-famous architect whose aesthetic style and creations are awe-inspiring. AKA, the only architects you've ever heard of: *Frank Lloyd Wright, Frank Gehry, and Le Corbusier are total starchitects I just deeply respect their work.*

staycation

noun / portmanteau

A vacation undertaken in your own town, or city, or general region; leisure time that does not involve travelling long distances. A chance for anyone to develop an appreciation for the offerings of your home environ.

STFU

abbreviation / initialism

Shut the fuck up.

streaming
verb
A method of accessing content via the internet as a flow of data, without having to download it first. Additionally, *live streaming* refers to the broadcast and consumption of various media online in real time: *Darren is live streaming baby Huxley's first nappy change! I've gotta get home and watch it!*

suh
interjection
Portmanteau of *sup* (the abbreviation of *what's up?*) and *huh*; an exclamation of excitement and confusion: *'Hey, man.' 'Suh, dude.'*

sus
abbreviation / adjective
Short for *suspect* or *suspicious*; shady situations or people whose words or actions aren't earning your trust: *I don't know about Brayden... dude seems kinda sus to me.*

swag
abbreviation / noun
Short for *swagger*; an expression of exterior confidence. A way of carrying yourself that suggests impressiveness, a look that exudes style, certainty, and success: *Rihanna has swag. Rihanna has swag in abundance. Rihanna has 17 truckloads of swag.* (See also: **BDE**.)

swerve
verb
To *swerve* is, obviously, to dodge or evade. Its most common usage now refers to dodging or evading another person. The origin of this usage can be traced back to the song 'Mercy' by Kanye West.

swol
abbreviation / adjective
Swol derives from the word 'swollen'. It means muscularity in today's context. If a person is described as 'swol' then they are someone who works out. Synonyms include 'jacked', 'built', or 'buff'.

synergy
noun
Combining forces for greater productivity and mutual understanding, AKA, *the* marketing buzzword of a couple of years ago, AKA, utterly meaningless.

T

TBH
initialism
Initialism of *to be honest*; a redundant and overused phrase employed by the inarticulate when attempting to cement a point. Often said aloud, in speech: *I didn't like that movie at all, TBH.*

TBQH
initialism
To be quite honest.

TBT
hashtag / initialism
Originally meaning 'throwback Thursday', *TBT* can also stand for 'throwback to'. This is a way of recalling the past, a good one to know when posting those nostalgic photos of your European vacation. (It's okay, we've all done it.)

TDTM
initialism
Talk dirty to me. Need we say more?

tea
noun
Hot gossip; the scoop. A term origination from *ye olde* times, where gossip would literally be shared over cups of piping hot tea. If you're hanging on to some good *tea*, it may be time to spill it.

techbro
noun
A person working in the field of technology. *Techbro* can also imply this person is a recluse, or generally lacking in social skills. The term also carries implications of arrogance and all-round assholery.

TFW
initialism
Meaning for 'That Feeling When', *TFW* is used almost as a prefix before a description of a common and/or relatable sentiment, emotion, or action: *TFW you leave work on a Friday afternoon...*

T

thank u, next
phrase
A sophisticated (well, okay, perhaps not all that sophisticated) way of telling somebody to 'fuck off'.
Paul: *'You know, you've got a real attitude problem.'*
Helen: *'Thank u, next.'*

the house down
phrase
With roots in drag culture, this phrase is used dropped at the end of a sentence to magnify the import of the overall sentiment: *Damn, Lizzo can twerk the house down.*

thicc
adjective
This alternative spelling of the word 'thick' is, like many words and phrases within this dictionary, contextually specific, as it refers to the dimensions of a person's body. To be 'thicc' is to be curvy, perhaps even... *bootylicious*...

thirst trap

noun

'Thirst' derives from 'thirsty' (see below) and 'trap', meaning to lure. On social media, a 'thirst trap' is any provocative image, photograph, or message posted online with the intention of drawing the thirsty to comment.

thirsty

adjective

For a time, this word had connotations of desperation. It still means desperate, in a certain kind of way... desperately horny.

THOT

acronym

'That Hoe Over There'. Used to describe anyone who is going over the top to attract a partner. Once a misogynistic slur used against women, now coopted to more widely describe anyone trying too hard.

throw hands

verb

When you're about to get into a fight, then you're about to 'throw hands'. *Keep talking smack and I'm gonna throw hands!* Yeah, best to never use this one...

T

thx / tnx
abbreviation / acronym
Thanks. A three-letter abbreviation for a six-letter word... Coz u've jst gtta fnd wys 2 sve tme!

TIA
initialism
Thanks in advance.

TIFU
initialism
Today I fucked up.

TIL
initialism
Today I learned.

time sink
noun
Something pointless into which you invest your time, which yields little (or no) results: *I probably shouldn't have binged EVERY season of* The Office *this week... bit of a time sink.*

Tinder flake
noun
Your average Tinder date... AKA a 'time sink'...

tl;dr
initialism
Online shorthand for *too long; didn't read*.
Used after longwinded chunks of text (or,
sometimes, anything over one paragraph)
to summarise the argument for us lazy skim
readers: *tl;dr it's an internet thing, okay?*

TMA
initialism
Take my advice.

TMI
initialism
Too much information. Like when Dad starts
telling everyone at the dinner table about his
latest prostate exam. Yeah, TMI.

TMYL
initialism
Text me your location.

tooch
verb

To *tooch* your booty is to push your derrière out while having your photograph taken, in order to accentuate your rump, to make it appear larger, plump, and more rounded.
A modelling technique popularised by Tyra Banks. (See also: **smize**.)

toxic masculinity
noun

A poisonous brand of performative, heteronormative behaviour that upholds the status quo, usually in service to the patriarchy and oppressive to any and all minority groups.
A real *boys will be boys*-type attitude; a real *bros before hoes*-type douchey vibe.

train wreck
noun

An unmitigated catastrophe or a complete and total disaster: *Ethan has been a train wreck ever since he got dumped by Emily.* Or: *That movie was a fucking train wreck from start to finish.*

transparency
noun
A corporate strategy buzzword; where a company allowa the public to see their inner machinations (or, some PR-devised approximation thereof) in order to be perceived as trustworthy.

trash
adjective
Anything that's just completely terrible (and hence would be better off being thrown away like garbage): *I hate taking the bus to work. Buses are trash.*

trigger warning
noun
Originally a term used by mental health professionals in relation to PTSD, the term today is used widely by publishing and media companies, as well as entertainment providers, as a signpost that some content could adversely affect people struggling with issues of mental health. (See also: **CW** and **UV**.)

trill
adjective / portmanteau
'Trill' combines the words 'true' and 'real' to give us a word enhancing the real and true meanings of both...

troll
noun
A person who intentionally sows discord on the internet by starting arguments and upsetting people. This is achieved by posting inflammatory, extraneous, or off-topic messages in comment sections and on social media, with the deliberate intent of provoking emotional responses from other users for the troll's own amusement. Essentially, everything that's bad about the internet.

true that
interjection
A term of agreement meaning 'that's right' or 'yup': *'I feel like Greg is just a fuckboi with decent fashion sense.' 'True that.'*

TTG
initialism
Time to go.

TTYL
initialism
Talk to you later.

turducken
noun / portmanteau
A culinary term referring to a roast dish consisting of a chicken stuffed inside a duck stuffed inside a turkey.

turnt
adjective
Amplified, intense; basically, the precursor to 'lit'. Can refer to a state of inebriation and/or being hyped up: *I was super turnt last night.* Or: *This party is fucking turnt.*

TWD
initialism
Texting while driving. This is about the last thing you'd want to admit to, not to mention how dumb you've gotta be to create a record of your illegal behavior, but... Well, no, there are no 'buts'!

twerk
verb
A dance move that involves a low squatting stance, ferocious hip-thrusting motions, and the rapid clapping together of one's asscheeks. The twenty-first century's answer to the Charleston.

TYS
initialism
Told you so. If this isn't the most obnoxious phrase already in existence, abbreviating it only makes it more so.

TYT
initialism
Take your time.

TYVM
initialism
Thank you very much. *You're welcome!*

U

U mad bro?
phrase
A redundant question deployed when you are aware that someone is mad, and you wish only to make them madder.

U up?
phrase
When you're up late at night and browsing your dating/hookup apps, someone is bound to ask, '*U up?*'. The real meaning? '*Send nudes!*' Or even: '*Wanna come over?*' Hey, at least they're interested... right?

UDI
initialism / noun
Unidentified drinking injury. Damage incurred to your body when so inebriated, you have no memory of it being sustained.

U

UFB
adjective / initialism
Un-fucking-believable.

UI
initialism / noun
Short for 'user interface'.

UK
initialism
No, this isn't shorthand for the United Kingdom. Well, it still is, of course. But online, UK might be an abbreviation of 'you know'. So, well, *you know...*

unboxing
verb
The act of removing a product from its packaging. Videos depicting people opening products, especially those made by Apple, are bizarrely popular on YouTube. These videos sometimes double as product reviews.

unspun
adjective
Lacking in spin, genuine, authentic;
commonly used in political discourse:
The voters are seriously desperate
for some unspun politics.

UOK
initialism
You okay?

upvote
noun / verb
The act of giving online content such as an
article, video, or post a positive rating. For
instance, hitting the 'like' button on a YouTube
video is to give that video an upvote.

ur
abbreviation
Short for both *your* and *you're*, which
makes this abbreviation a rather irritating
one for those insistent on preserving the
English language.

U

UTM
initialism
You tell me.

UV
initialism / noun
Once upon a time, someone mentioning the letters UV would've meant they were talking about ultraviolet radiation. Well, in the online world, forget sun safety, because today UV means 'unpleasant visual'. (See also: **CW** and **trigger warning**.)

V

v
abbreviation / adjective / adverb
Short for very: I just really don't think
Ron is a v good influence on Hermione.

vaping
verb
Inhaling vapour from an e-cig or a vape; analogous
to smoking, but instead the substance inhaled and
exhaled is vapour, not smoke. The term applies
both to vaping nicotine and dry-herb vaping
(smoking cannabis).

Vaporwave
noun
A music genre and art/design movement that emerged
in the early 2010s out of genres such as seapunk,
bounce house, witch house, and chillwave. Vaporwave
is characterised by a fascination with nostalgic and
surrealist retro cultural aesthetics and styles.

V

victim blaming / shaming
verb
The act of bringing shame or blame upon someone who is a victim (as opposed to blaming their attacker) in a way that implies the victim deserved or somehow caused their attack, by way of harassment, usually in a verbal and/or online context.

viewability
noun
The degree to which something is able to be seen or watched or looked at by a mass audience or specific demographic, incorporating also the degree to which that audience will find the visual content stimulating and/or agreeable.

viral
adjective / noun
Content that explodes in popularity and reaches a mass audience within a very short time period. The Holy Grail for digital marketers: *All we need for this campaign to succeed is for this tweet to go viral.*

VPN
initialism
Standing for 'virtual private network', a VPN is a sneaky way around any internet filters you might come across. So long as you're tech savvy enough to know how it all works, of course...

W

W8
abbreviation
Wait.

wake 'n bake
verb
To wake up and smoke cannabis. *Bake* is a derivative of the word *baked*, which is slang for stoned or high. The phrase is a reference to a breadcrumb-style food product called Shake 'n Bake. (But now 'shake 'n bake' has been co-opted to mean 'cooking meth', so...)

wat?
abbreviation
What? There's been a few changes to the spelling of basic words in recent times, and here's yet another example. It's just wat is happening right now. So *wat*? (We also accept 'wut' and 'wot' as replacements of the very archaic word 'what'.)

WB
initialism
Welcome back. A way to greet someone back to the chat room, or group chat.

#WCW
hashtag / initialism
Initialism for *Woman* (or *Women*) *Crush Wednesday*; an attachment to a social media post, published on a Wednesday, about a woman you have a non-romantic crush on, generally with the intention to highlight and celebrate her impressive achievements.

we out here
phrase
Attributed to Californian skateboarding legend Larry Redmon, that speaks to 'the hustle' or 'the struggle'. It's used to signal that someone is hard at work: *Yeah, we out here, slinging these girl-guide cookies. #fundraiser*

weird flex
verb
Adding a twist to the new meaning of 'flex', a *weird flex* is to brag about something that one really shouldn't be proud of, or something that no one cares about. It raises the question, *Why would they tell me that?* (See also: **flex**.)

wellness
noun
State of being after making good choices that have led to an overall healthy lifestyle; now co-opted by deranged health obsessives who happily promote outlandish (and/or scientifically unfounded) methods to achieve a Nirvana-like state of *wellness*.

WFM
initialism
Works for me.

What's good?
phrase
Simply put, this is another way of asking, 'What's been happening?' or, 'What's up?'

wheelhouse
noun
Someone's field of knowledge or area of expertise; what you know, understand, or are most capable of doing: *You want a definitive listing of Mandy Moore's top five movie roles? That is so totally in my wheelhouse.* Or: *Sorry, Snapchat is just completely outside my wheelhouse.*

whip
noun
A car, or ride. Supposedly, when cars were first manufactured, the steering wheel was referred to as the 'whip', as whips were the steering mechanism for a stagecoach. Noting that the Mercedes Benz logo looks like a steering wheel, hip-hop artists began referring to Mercedes as *whips*. The term has now come to refer to any car or ride.

white knighting
verb
The act of coming to a person's 'rescue' when the act of rescue is unwanted and/ or unwarranted; involving yourself in someone else's situation in a thoughtless and intrusive manner.

wicked
adjective / adverb
Very, really, extremely; but be warned, when using wicked you must always put on a terrible Boston accent. Examples include *wicked smart* (really smart), *wicked cool* (really cool), *wicked chill* (very relaxed) and *wicked hot* (super sexy or sexy as hell).

wig
exclamation
Like the term 'shook', this word denotes surprise and disbelief, usually with positive connotations. It is derived from the phrase 'my wig flew off' and is used when a person is shocked by something: *'I'm FINALLY doing it! I've signed up to a pottery class.' 'OMG. No way, girl! Wig!'*

wig snatched
verb
Much like 'wig', *wig snatched* refers to someone being so shocked or surprised by something that they have lost their wig. Another variation of the phrase, however, can refer to the act of exposing a person to reveal the truth about their character.

Wiki-hole
noun
The loss of time associated with looking up something on Wikipedia and being dragged Into a black hole of unrelated links and new, and increasingly unrelated, information: *I jumped on Wikipedia to find out Timothée Chalamet's age, but wound up in a Wiki-hole about the Russian Revolution.*

wind it down
verb
To calm down or curb your enthusiasm; to lower the tone of something, most especially your state of being: *Jace was losing his shit over finding some Pokémon. I had to ask him to wind it down.*

win–win
noun
A scenario where, no matter what happens, the outcome will be positive. Generally, implies you must make a choice between two or more options, and all choices will lead to a positive result. (See also: **lose–lose**.)

WK
abbreviation
Week. Go on, you know you've always wanted to lose those worthless double e's...

woke
adjective
Aware, relevant, ahead of the trends; if you want to stay cool and up (or is it down?) with the zeitgeist, then you need to stay *woke*, which is exactly what this handy book is for: *Stay woke, fam.*

word
interjection
Correct, positive affirmation; expression of agreement with the words and sentiment being spoken by a second party: *'That Kendrick Lamar track is fire.' 'Word.'*

WRT
initialism
With regard to.

WTF
initialism
If you don't know what this stands for by now, we're not going to help you on this one. What the fuck are you doing this far into the book if you don't even know what *WTF* means? *WTF?*

WTG
initialism
Way to go. One of the scant initialisms that can easily retain its sarcasm when read.

W

WTH
initialism
What the hell?

WYCM
initialism
Will you call me? Sounds a bit lonely and desperate now, doesn't it? You should probably call them.

WYD
initialism
Meaning 'What You Doing?', *WYD* is a great shorthand for those searching for a booty call. No question mark is needed, of course; the implication speaks its own volumes.

WYWH
initialism
Wish you were here. *Aww...*

x / xx / xo / xox
noun

Kisses and hugs. Today, signing off with a kiss or a hug has become so ubiquitous that people even include them in work emails: *Thanks for getting that transcript to us in time, Jen. You're a star! xxox*

xennial
noun

A *xennial* refers to older millennials, those born between 1977 and 1983. Xennials didn't get Facebook until well after high school, and they're a little touchy about being lumped in with the likes of Lena Dunham, so they now need their own identity. Because that's not overly sensitive at all, is it?

xenophobia
noun

The irrational fear or dislike of people from other countries. While this certainly isn't a modern word, the proliferation of its usage is current and completely fucking terrifying.

Y

yas / yass / yaas
exclamation
Alternative spelling of yes. One morning the internet woke up and decided to replace the 'e' with an 'a' and the world hasn't been the same since... The amount of s's and a's can vary, but you get the general idea.

yass queen
interjection
A statement of affirmation and excitement in celebration of someone or something. A phrase the internet and wider world coopted from people of colour (more specifically, queer people of colour). Spelling varies wildly, with the user adding as many a's and s's as they see fit: *'I got the job!' 'YaAAaasSsss KWEEN!'*

yeet
exclamation / verb
A way of expressing nervous excitement, pure joy, or even agreement; vaguely akin to 'yay': *Yeet!* Also used to describe the act of throwing something at high velocity: *Oh fuck... Lewis just yeeted his phone out the window.*

YMMD
initialism
You made my day.

YMMV
initialism
Initialism of *your mileage may vary*; most commonly used in online forums as an acknowledgement that the opinion of the 'poster' may not be shared by everyone.

YOLO
acronym / phrase
You only live once; the *carpe diem* for the stupidest among us and *the* motto of the internet in 2011. Somehow, it's still clinging on. The phrase has come to be used as an excuse for any misguided action: *This credit card might send me into an irreversible spiral of debt, but... YOLO fam.*

YouTuber
noun
A person who makes their living by publishing regular videos on YouTube. These videos, usually but certainly not always, are either aspirational or somewhat instructional, with a specific focus on some lifestyle aspect, whether health, fashion, or beauty, or the arts and comedy.

yup
exclamation
Alternative spelling of *yep*, which is itself an alternative to *yes*. So... *yup*.

yuppie
abbreviation / noun
The young, urban professional never went away. Right? Now they're drinking Aperol Spritzes and hitting the cafes for bougie brunches. They like their kombucha now, too. But except for the modern trappings, they haven't really changed much...

Z

-z
suffix

Used to make any word awesome by its simple inclusion; commonly used in place of the letter 's' where it is used to denote a plural, or just whereever: *Hey babez! Damn you serve some lookz. Don't worry about what she said, haterz gonna try and take down your dreamz.*

za
noun

Short for pizza; an abbreviation popular with males of the frat and or fuckboi variety. Employment of the term is mostly ironic, with the implication being that those who use it sincerely are essentially braindead: *Duuuuuuude. We getting a whole za or just a slice??*

zaddy
noun

A term for a fashionable and handsome older man. Any *zaddy* worth his salt oozes sex appeal, and can probably afford to buy you a second (and third) copy of this book.

Z

zero chill
adjective
To be completely lacking in chill; not relaxed; uptight, nervous, anxious, or in any way uncool: *Kim Jong-un has, like, zero chill. He has, like, negative chill.*

zing
interjection
An exclamation you make after you've said something particularly witty, and you'd really like to point out to everyone just how witty you've been.

zomg
interjection
A variant of OMG, meaning 'oh my god!'; the alternate version to be used in contexts where the intention of OMG is sarcastic or to highlight that someone has stated the obvious: *Trickle-down economics doesn't work?? ZOMG! No fucking way!*

One More Thing

Well. It's been a wild linguistic ride, hasn't it? I sincerely hope your lexicon is now comparable to that of any 14-year-old with a smartphone. I also hope that you're not left dwelling on how principles of grammar, forged and refined over centuries, have been systematically tossed aside since the dawn of digital communication. It's better to just let that slide, TBQH.

To conclude *A Very Modern Dictionary*, I wanted to point out some rules of grammar and syntax this book adheres to. Most importantly, I should mention that throughout these pages I've upheld the distinction between acronym and initialism – whose vast difference is too often overlooked, and is a hill upon which I will gladly die. Please indulge me...

Acronyms and initialisms are two very similar forms of abbreviation. Acronyms take the initial letters from a series of words to make an entirely new word (FOMO and THOT, for example). Initialisms, which are more common, instead pronounce each letter separately (like AF or WTF). To further muddy these waters, sometimes an abbreviation can swing both ways, functioning as either an acronym or initialism depending on the personal preference of the speaker. LOL and ASAP are examples of these pesky abbreviations. Although, if you know anyone who spells out L-O-L in everyday speech then you may want to distance yourself.

Other entries in this book are classified as abbreviations when they are just shortened words (awks and obvi, for example). Then I have pointed out when other entries function as adjectives, nouns or verbs, in cases where the distinction is necessary for clarity.

As you might have already guessed, I am using this disclaimer to avoid the fiery wrath of nitpicking pedants who might otherwise send lengthy emails of complaint. They will likely do so anyway, but it's worth a try.

Tobias.

Published in 2020 by Smith Street Books
Melbourne | Australia
smithstreetbooks.com

ISBN: 978-1-925811-36-0

Publisher: Paul McNally
Project editor: Patrick Boyle
Designer: Murray Batten
Design layout: Heather Menzies, Studio 31 Graphics
Proofreader: Jack Calil

Printed & bound in China by C&C Offset Printing Co., Ltd.

Book 110
10 9 8 7 6 5 4 3 2 1